NANCY CHAMBERS

RIVER SPEY CANOE GUIDE

A CANOEIST AND KAYAKER'S GUIDE TO SCOTLAND'S PREMIER TOURING RIVER

First published 2014

Published in Great Britain 2014 by Pesda Press

Tan y Coed Canol

Ceunant

Caernarfon

Gwynedd

LL55 4RN

Copyright © 2014 Nancy Chambers

ISBN   978-1-906095-43-7

The Author asserts the moral right to be identified as the author of this work.

All rights reserved. No part of this publication may be reproduced, stored in a retrieval system, or transmitted, in any form or by any means, electronic, mechanical, photocopying, recording or otherwise, without the prior written permission of the Publisher.

Maps by Bute Cartographic.

Printed and bound in Poland, www.hussarbooks.pl

Foreword

At first fed by only trickling ditches high in the Monadhliath Mountains, then by larger tributaries including the Feshie and Avon, the River Spey gathers momentum as it moves toward sharing its fresh waters with Moray Firth brine.

Scotland's fastest flowing river, stretching for almost 100 miles through beautiful Highland countryside, this natural water path has for centuries been navigated by various forms of floating craft. From the mid-1780s, great trunks from the ancient Forest of Caledon were floated downstream in rafts guided by skilled loggers who risked life and limb manhandling these behemoths to shipyards at Garmouth.

On a smaller scale the locals sculled currachs, constructed of a wooden frame covered by stretched skins. These saucer-like boats needed skill to control, and were used to carry small items or to visit neighbours perhaps situated on the far bank.

In the 20th century log rafts and currachs were replaced by kayaks. Then, in the 1980s came open canoes, probably the most ideal craft for journeying on major Scottish rivers.

Ever-changing scenery surrounds the Spey on its journey to the sea. Cradled first between the Monadhliath and Grampian Mountains, the mighty Spey then meanders through flat agricultural lands towards Grantown. After the majesty of thick forested banks throughout Moray comes the shingle flats from Fochabers to the sea. Proficient paddlers can safely enjoy descents of up to 70 miles. Under terms of Land Reform (Scotland) Act 2003, much of the Spey has formal 'Core Path' designation.

The Scottish Canoe Association website carries an informative but informal paddlers' guide to the Spey. However, given the Spey's iconic status in terms of canoe touring, there has been an obvious need for a thoroughly comprehensive publication. Here in this book, Nancy has creatively produced an expansive guide which will help the reader gain better understanding of the River Spey, and facilitate their enjoyment of this majestic water path – without doubt, Britain's most beautiful canoe touring river.

Dave Craig
SCOTTISH CANOE ASSOCIATION ADVISER (RIVER SPEY) 1981 TO PRESENT
(For further information on canoe/access matters relating to the River Spey contact Dave Craig on 01540 673826 or dave@spiritofthespey.co.uk)

Contents

Foreword 3
Contents 4
Introduction 7
The author 8
Acknowledgements 9

Planning your River Journey 13

Ability and group 13
Shuttles 14
Equipment and packing 15
Suggested paddling kit list 18
Weather and river levels 19

The River Spey

The Upper River – Loch Spey to Lochain Uvie 23
Suggested itineraries 27
Section 1 – Lochain Uvie to Loch Insh 31
Section 2 – Loch Insh to Aviemore 37
Section 3 – Aviemore to Boat of Balliefurth 41
Section 4 – Boat of Balliefurth to Cragganmore ... 47
Section 5 – Cragganmore to Craigellachie 53
Section 6 – Craigellachie to Spey Bay 61

Safety and Rescue 67

Access, Wild Camping and Fishing 69
    Wild camping 69
    Toileting 70
    Campfires 70
    Fishing 71

Wildlife 75
    In the water 75
    On the land 77
    In the air 79

Environmental Issues 83

History of the River Spey 85
    Logging 85
    Whisky and distilleries 86
    Railways 86
    Farming and droving 87
    Salmon fishing at Spey Bay 87

Navigation skills for the River 89
    Grid references 89
    Using features to identify where you are 91
    Relocation skills 91

Index 92

Below Aberlour.

Introduction

The River Spey is one of the classic open canoe journeys in the UK. That said, it is increasingly popular with touring kayaks, and if broken down into day trips is very enjoyable in whitewater river kayaks and inflatable canoes. The Spey has stretches of flat water and lochs, gentle moving water and exciting grade 2 rapids. It can be paddled as a complete journey or, if using the agreed access and egress points, can be broken down into superb day paddles. The Spey starts its journey high in the mountains at Loch Spey, and flows and tumbles its way down to the Spey Dam and then across a flatter area passing Laggan village, and down past Lochain Uvie where we start the river description. It then flows down to the sea passing many villages and beautiful rural spots on the way.

There are usually many wonderful wildlife sightings when on the river, ranging from ospreys to dippers, otters and salmon. The wild flowers on the riverbank in summer make a beautiful display, and the fishing huts particularly in the mid to lower sections of the river are manicured to perfection, showing a great diversity in river usage throughout.

The journey down the River Spey from Lochain Uvie to Spey Bay is 135 kilometers and passes over three OS 1:50,000 map sheets, 35 Kingussie and the Monadhliath Mountains, 36 Grantown and Aviemore, and 28 Elgin, Dufftown and surrounding area. It is a stunning journey to complete and should be a must on every paddler's tick list.

The author

Nancy is a passionate paddler who is most at home in her canoe. She is also regularly found in a sea kayak and occasionally in a white water kayak. Multi-day journeys are her favourite personal adventure, especially if they are spent on the water with her family and friends.

She has spent her career working in the outdoors and currently works for half her time as an instructor for Glenmore Lodge, the National Outdoor Training Centre, where you will find her delivering a range of paddlesport and mountaineering courses. In addition to this Nancy works for other organisations and occasionally runs bespoke guided or training course for groups. She holds a range of high level outdoor qualifications including the BCU Level 5 Canoe Coach award and enjoys most other outdoor sports.

Nancy visited the Aviemore area as a child and has many happy memories of her holidays here. In her late teens she returned to work as a ski instructor, then moved to the west coast of Scotland before returning to live near Aviemore in 2002. She has been paddling on the River Spey since 1990, when she was introduced to its beauty on a staff training trip from Lowport Outdoor Education Centre. Since then she has paddled regularly in the area and all around Scotland.

Nancy Chambers paddling on Loch Spey. Photo | Nick March.

Acknowledgements

There are lots of people to thank for their help during the writing and photo taking for this book. Doug Cooper for helping with the initial idea. Dave Craig for being a great font of knowledge on the river. Franco and Vicky at Pesda Press. Donald Macpherson for helping with photos and information about writing a book. Alison Faulconbridge for helping with the photos and just being great craic on the river. Tom and Kate Oxtoby for being models for photos and reading my writing prior to sending it to Franco. Karl and Carol Atherton for suggestions on the upper section. The many landowners and ghillies that I have chatted to on and about the river. The many folks I have paddled with over the years on the Spey who have increased the enthusiasm that I have for the river, and who have been models for the pictures. The biggest thanks need to go to my family, Nick, Olly and Eddy, who have helped and supported me by giving me the time to complete the project, being willing models on the river, and taking some photos as well. If I have missed someone out apologies and many thanks for your help.

All photos taken by Nancy Chambers unless acknowledged in the caption.

Important notice – disclaimer

Canoeing and kayaking whether in a loch, river or sea environment has its inherent risks as do all adventurous activities. This guidebook highlights some considerations to take into account when planning your own river journey.

While we have included a range of factors to consider, you will need to plan your own journey and within that ensure there is scope to be adaptable to local tides, weather conditions and ever changing river hazards. This requires knowing your own abilities, then applying your own risk assessment to the conditions that you may encounter. The varying environmental conditions within the river and its lochs means that every day good judgement is required to decide whether to paddle or not.

The information within this book has been well researched, however neither the author, nor Pesda Press can be held responsible for any decision of whether to paddle or not and any consequences arising from that decision.

Paddling past Orton earth pillars.

Paddlers stopping at the fishing weir in Grantown.

Planning your River Journey

Whether it's a one-day trip with novices, or a multi-day adventure with experienced paddlers, thorough planning can make all the difference to your paddling adventure. Carrying the right kit, knowing the best campsites and checking the weather forecast will help make your river journey an enjoyable experience, for everyone!

Ability and group

When you are planning your journey down the River Spey you first of all need to think about your own ability and that of the group that you are going with. If you are planning to do the whole river as novices and have limited experience, you should consider joining a guided or instructional group to complete the journey. There are some sections of the river where there is little flow and the rapids are easy to negotiate, so if you are less experienced you can have a great day out on these sections without a guide or instructor. If you are happy paddling on grade 2 moving water then a fully self-guided trip may be appropriate for you.

If you go with the guided option, a suitably qualified guide or instructor will make the journey a memorable experience for you. They should know all the best campsites, know the best places to play on the river, and in the event of a mishap be able to sort it out, including dealing with any capsizes, changes to plans, shuttles and so on. They may also organise your boat, paddles, equipment and food for the journey, allowing you to just turn up and enjoy the river.

If you are organising your own group a suggested maximum number of boats in one group would be six or seven, although a more manageable group size would be three or

Group leaving the access point at Ballindalloch.

four boats. Some people don't like paddling in groups, and for them solo paddling (or paddling a single tandem boat) is the preferred option. If you choose to paddle with just one boat, then you must be aware of the additional risks involved. If you are paddling on your own and you capsize, then your only option is to self-rescue, which is a reasonably advanced skill and requires a good level of knowledge and skill base. If you are leading a group of friends on the river in the BCU scheme, the minimum level of skill and experience suggested would be a 4 Star Leader in your chosen craft. It is essential that at least one member of the group knows what to do in the event of an emergency on the river, and has the appropriate safety equipment with them to deal with a pinned or capsized boat and crew, and they should really explain this to the rest of the group prior to departing on the river.

Completing the descent of the River Spey can be done as either day trips with a shuttle for each section, which means that you can paddle a light boat, or you can set off for the full journey with all of your camping and paddling equipment. This latter option means that you will have to carry everything in your boat, which makes it much heavier and potentially less manoeuvrable. This is a skill in itself, and if you have not paddled a fully laden boat before it is worth practising your river skills (breaking in and out and ferry gliding) with all of your kit in the boat prior to your trip.

Shuttles

At some point you will have to move yourself and your boat around. If you can organise enough cars to be in the area, it will take you just under 2 hours to drive to Spey Bay from Newtonmore. You are asked not to leave cars overnight at the car park at Tugnet, but you can leave your vehicle in the campsite at the Spey Bay Golf Club if you are going to camp there after your trip. Contact them directly to arrange leaving your vehicle there on 01343 820424.

There are a number of operators who provide shuttles if doing the whole river; all offer a shuttle service with a minibus and trailer:

Johnny's Taxis 01479 851375

Explore Highland info@explorehighland.com or 0780 807 1810

Boots N Paddles info@canoehirescotland.co.uk or 0845 612 5567

If completing your shuttle by public transport, you need to walk from Spey Bay to Garmouth over the viaduct. From Garmouth you can get a bus to Elgin (there are a few buses direct from Spey Bay, but more from Garmouth). You can then get either a bus or train to Inverness. From Inverness you can get either a bus or train to Aviemore, Kingussie or Newtonmore; depending on connections it will take around 4 to 6 hours.

An idea for a novel shuttle service, if you are paddling from Aviemore to Broomhill with one or two boats, is to ask the Strathspey Steam Railway on 01479 810725 in advance if they will carry your boat back to Aviemore in the guard's van. If they have space they are usually very accommodating.

Equipment and packing

The classic craft of those completing a descent of the River Spey is a canoe, because you can fit a large amount of equipment into the boat with ease. Many people are now using touring kayaks, and certainly for day trips a whitewater river kayak is suitable. There has also been an increase in the number of inflatable canoes (duckies) that are paddling on the river. Whichever craft you choose make sure that it is river worthy and that you have a repair kit for it before you go.

Packing a canoe

Once you have decided what to take with you, it is important to be able to keep it all dry and to fit it all into your craft. Barrels and dry bags are the usual way of doing this. There are a variety of sizes of both available. If you use barrels you would normally be able to take two or three barrels per boat. Two 60 litre barrels will usually fit into most 16 foot boats side by

Packing a canoe.

Preparing for the journey ahead.

side, and you can often fit in a third, smaller, 30 litre barrel in front of that.

If you are using dry bags, ensure they are closed properly, and it is worth double bagging items that you need to keep dry, such as your sleeping bag. There are a number of good dry bag rucksacks and carry bags on the market at the moment. Again two of these will normally fit into a 16 foot canoe. You can then have your day bag with essentials in it easily accessible on top or in front of you.

In a tandem canoe, if taking three barrels you will usually choose to have one barrel each for personal kit, and one for communal kit and food.

Once you have got all your kit into your barrels or bags you need to decide how to tie them into your boat. My preferred method is to tie them in so they won't move in the boat as there is no loose line to get tangled up in should you capsize. The down side to this is that if you have to rescue the boat it makes it very heavy to lift, despite reducing the volume of water that you can get into the boat. Using this method means that in all cases the bags or barrels stay with the boat if there is a problem. I usually keep my day bag on a loose line, which is the other method of tying equipment in. The pros to this method are that you can move kit around more easily, and if you capsize you can just empty the water out of the boat and then bring the barrels or bags back in board. The down side is that there is rope floating around in the boat/water which could cause an entanglement. If you use this method make sure you tie a releasable knot so you can get rid of the bags if necessary. There are others who advocate not tying in bags at

Tracking on the Upper River Spey. Photo | Nick March.

all so there are no entanglement issues. If you choose not to tie your bags in at all, then please be very aware that your kit can get lost if you capsize, and you may need it, especially if it is the communal barrel with tent, stove and food in it.

Packing a touring kayak

In a touring kayak you have slightly less space than in a canoe, so you might have to be a bit more ruthless with your packing list, but you usually have plenty of space to pack a few non-essentials in the hatches as well.

Each touring kayak will have a number of dry hatches for you to pack kit into. I always make sure that any kit that must stay dry is properly sealed in a dry bag. When you are packing your touring kayak, you need to think about the trim of your boat. Normally you want the bow of your boat to be slightly lighter than the stern. So I will often put heavier items such as food, tent and stove in the rear hatch and pack additional, softer stuff such as clothes around it. The bow hatch usually contains lighter items such as sleeping mat, sleeping bag, and clothes.

There will be some items that you will need regularly, and you might want to put some smaller ones in your buoyancy aid pocket or in the cockpit of your boat. If you are carrying water rather than filtering it, I normally carry this in the cockpit as well to keep the trim more neutral, and to avoid any unnoticed leakages onto clothes or other important items. Please be aware that any items that are free in the cockpit may float away if you capsize. You should also check your hatches before the trip to ensure that they are watertight.

Suggested paddling kit list

Paddling kit
- Boat with airbags
- Paddle
- Spare paddle
- Bailer and sponge
- Painter and swim lines (canoe)
- Sail and poles (canoe)
- Spray deck (kayak only)
- Day bag or rucksack for use as a day bag

Personal equipment
- Buoyancy aid with whistle and river knife
- Paddling clothes and good footwear
- Helmet
- Knee pads or kneeling mats (for canoes)

Camping equipment
Personal
- Clothes, shoes, hat and gloves
- Toiletries and towel, including any personal medication
- Sleeping bag and mat
- Lunch bag, water bottle and flask (in day bag/easy access)
- Plate, mug, knife, fork and spoon
- Sun cream and midge repellent (in day bag/easy access)

Shared
- Tent
- Stove, fuel, lighter and cooking pots
- Water carrier and optional filter/purifier (if planning to use river water to drink)
- Toilet paper, trowel and zip lock bags
- Rubbish bags

Day bag/easy access items
- Map and compass and GPS if carried
- Mobile phone (although you may wish to carry this in your buoyancy aid)
- Lunch and snack food
- Flask/water bottle
- First aid kit
- Group shelter and survival bag
- Spare clothes in the event of capsize/feeling cold
- Sun cream, sun hat and sunglasses

Safety equipment
- Rescue kit (slings, karabiners, pulleys, prussics, etc) within easy access in the boat or on your person in a bum bag
- Throw bag
- First aid kit
- Map, compass and GPS (in day bag/easy access)
- Group shelter and survival bag (in day bag/easy access)
- Boat repair kit (duck tape, patches, two-part plumber's putty, spare bolts, adjustable spanner and screwdrivers or multi tool, lashing cord, cable ties, Aquasure or Freesole glue for airbag repairs)
- Mobile phone in a waterproof case, with enough charge for the length of journey you are planning (in day bag/easy access)
- Torch and spare batteries
- Radio/weather app on your phone (for weather reports)

Weather and river levels

When we are journeying on the river it is very important for us to know what the weather will be doing and consequently what the river levels will be like. River levels can change very quickly if there is heavy rain in the area of one or more of the main tributaries. This can turn the River Spey from a gentle river into a raging torrent without eddies and with large tree debris. Check your forecast before you go and keep your eye on the actual weather as you are out on the river.

Weather forecasts

The River Spey gets predominantly south-westerly winds. This is great as the river generally runs in a north-easterly direction so you often get the wind following you. It also means that the majority of the rain has already fallen on the West Coast and we are in the rain shadow here in the North East. However a large portion of the river's catchment area is to the west of us, or in the Cairngorms itself, and this can mean that the river levels can go up very quickly if there is a large amount of rainfall in the mountains. You can get weather forecasts that will tell you about the wind direction, rainfall and temperature from many sources. The internet is an amazing source of information and can localise forecasts for the different villages on the river. Try www.xcweather.co.uk, www.bbc.co.uk/weather, www.metoffice.gov.uk and www.mwis.org.uk as starting points.

Garva bridge in lowish water. Photo | Nick March.

Touring kayaks near Ballindalloch.

If you do not have access to a computer or smartphone then you can get information in a more traditional way through the radio. BBC Radio Scotland has good weather information in its 'out of doors' forecast Monday to Friday 1904hrs, Saturday 0704hrs and 2204hrs and Sunday 0704hrs and 2004hrs.

River levels

To get river levels there is a great website for paddlers called www.wheresthewater.com. This has a reading for the River Spey at Boat o' Brig. To get an indicator of what is happening above Aviemore then also have a look at the River Feshie levels. The Feshie is one of the main tributaries and can be a good indicator to the River Spey rising and falling. If there has been a lot of rain in the Cairngorms then it arrives into the river from the Feshie, the Druie, the Nethy and the Avon. If there has been a lot of rain on the west or in the Monadhliath then it arrives higher up from the Calder and from the Dulnain. Lower down the river you get a lot of water coming in from the Fiddich. Other good sources of information are www.fishpal.com, search for the River Spey where you can get river data all the way down, although on this site it is not interpreted for paddlers. Both of these websites get their information from the Scottish Environment Protection Agency (SEPA) which collects river level data on a daily basis.

If the calibration on the www.wheresthewater.com website is used, anything above a low level is a great fun run. On a medium to high level, or above, think carefully about whether you should get on the river, as there are few eddies and you can often get large tree debris coming down the river with you. If you have a capsize you can travel a long way down the river when you are sorting out a rescue, which can result in boats and people being a long distance apart.

In the summer the river will often be sitting at a low or scrape level but it is still possible to paddle the whole journey. However you may have to start further down the river at Loch Insh, which is a good holding point for the water, or even further down at Aviemore.

Autumn colours on the Spey.

📷 *Garva Bridge at low water.*

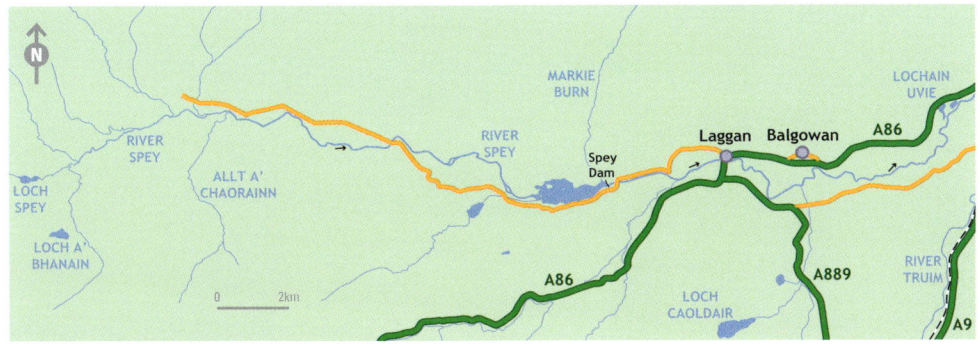

Upper River

The Upper River
Loch Spey to Lochain Uvie

The upper part of the river, above the more usual Lochain Uvie start, is best paddled in medium to high water. There are some rapids up to grade 3 on the section to the Spey Dam. At higher levels these can get up to grade 4 around Garva Bridge (the first major rapid starts at the corner of the forest plantation at NN 503 946). From Spey Dam down is grade 1(+).

The River Spey is a majestic river sweeping gracefully from its source in the Monadhliath Mountains, passing gently through the plains of Strathspey, and then picking up speed as it tumbles down to Spey Bay in Moray. It is a famous river in many rights from the salmon fishing, whisky distilling and paddling, to the interesting and rare wildlife sights that you see when travelling through on a journey down the Spey.

Loch Spey, high in the Monadhliath Mountains, is usually recognised to be the source of the Spey, although you could pick any of the many mountain burns that tumble down into the loch itself as being the true source. The river has been paddled from Loch Spey, however it takes a long walk with your boat and a lot of water to make it a viable option. There is a track leading to Glen Roy from Laggan that follows the river. As you travel along this track in a north-easterly direction from Loch Spey you see the river gaining in width and volume, as more small burns collect together and feed it. The river, more burn here, twists back and forth until it gains a little more maturity. There are some smaller rapids to contend with, and then some bigger ones (around grade 3) near Garva Bridge. The river

Grade 3 section on the upper river.

continues flowing through farmland down to the loch just above Spey Dam, where the water has been dammed to form a small loch in the beautiful mountainous surroundings. Water from here is piped away and diverted to the aluminium works in Fort William. It generally takes a lot of rain to open the Spey Dam to any significant amount. Passing round the dam you are into a more open section of river where it needs to be raining quite hard to keep the water flowing deep enough to paddle. Here the river takes on a wider outlook, with the tree-lined banks camouflaging the mountains that surround you. As you travel down towards Laggan village you get into a flatter section of river with the banks built up around you to reduce flooding. There have been recent flooding problems with the A86 near Laggan (on the drive between Aviemore and Fort William). There are many suggested solutions to this problem, but currently the main road has been limited to a single track road while they devise a permanent solution. In the winter months, it is not unusual to be driving with a big expanse of water either side of you when the river has flooded. To the north of Laggan Bridge is the first recognised access point on the river (NN 615 942), on the river right below the road bridge. This leads you in normal summer levels into a tree-lined, gravel-banked maze, where you often have to jump out of your boat to wade down sections, or pull across gravel banks before you get into the flow of the river. The banks here are raised up to try to alleviate flooding from the farmlands of the strath. Beyond this initial section the river deepens and you can paddle generally unhindered. As you meander down through the area you get some fine views of the Monadhliath Mountains and down towards the Glen Feshie hills with the Cairngorms in the distance. Once you start seeing the dark, imposing crags at Creag Dhubh on your left, you know that you are getting towards the more normal put-in points on the river. Even so, don't expect to see many other paddlers as far up as this, as most folks will choose to start at Newtonmore, Loch Insh or Aviemore, depending on how many days they have to spend on the river. See the suggested itineraries. Lochain Uvie near Creag Dhubh is the next put-in point here, and you will often share a car park with climbers intent on getting in some of the hard Creag Dhubh routes. If you are a keen hill walker, you can also walk from here to the top of Creag Dhubh to get a superb panorama taking in most of the strath towards Laggan, and with views northwards towards Aviemore. There is a herd of wild goats in this area that is worth looking out for as they clamber precariously about putting us humans to shame.

Between here and the sea the river has many major tributaries, the first being the Calder, followed by the Tromie, Feshie, Druie, Dulnain, Avon and several smaller rivers and burns as well, all of which have their sources in the major hills that surround the Spey. The fact that there is so much potential for water to run into the Spey is one of the reasons that it is so popular as a paddling river, as it is very rare that the river is too low to paddle.

Heading down river near Loch Spey. Photo | Nick March.

Water weed in bloom on the river.

Suggested Itineraries

This obviously depends on how far you would like to paddle in a day, but most folks can paddle between 20 and 30km per day without too many problems; the fitter you are the further you can go in a day. You may choose to paddle more or less depending on whether you want to explore the area further or want to have your head down and paddle hard. I have used three of the main starting points for the journey as being Lochain Uvie, Loch Insh and Aviemore. In higher water conditions the flow rate will be faster and you will find it easier travelling bigger distances.

From Lochain Uvie to Spey Bay is 135km, from Kincraig church to Spey Bay is 111km, and from Aviemore to Spey Bay is nearly 100km.

Most of these itineraries start and finish near recognised campsites; however, it is possible to wild camp near the river in many places. Please use sustainable practices if you are going to wild camp.

Suggestions for a 5-day trip

Option 1

Day	From	To	Distance (km)
1	Lochain Uvie	Kincraig church	24.0
2	Kincraig church	Boat of Balliefurth	32.4
3	Boat of Balliefurth	Cragganmore	27.0
4	Cragganmore	Craigellachie	22.4
5	Craigellachie	Spey Bay	29.2

Option 2

Day	From	To	Distance (km)
1	Kincraig church	Aviemore	11.3
2	Aviemore	Boat of Balliefurth	21.1
3	Boat of Balliefurth	Cragganmore	27.0
4	Cragganmore	Craigellachie	22.4
5	Craigellachie	Spey Bay	29.2

SUGGESTED ITINERARIES

Suggestions for a 4-day trip

Option 1

Day	From	To	Distance (km)
1	Lochain Uvie	Aviemore	35.3
2	Aviemore	Cromdale	30.6
3	Cromdale	Craigellachie	39.9
4	Craigellachie	Spey Bay	29.2

Option 2

Day	From	To	Distance (km)
1	Aviemore	Boat of Balliefurth	21.1
2	Boat of Balliefurth	Craggan-more	27.0
3	Craggan-more	Craigellachie	22.4
4	Craigellachie	Spey Bay	29.2

Option 3

Day	From	To	Distance (km)
1	Kingcraig church	Boat of Balliefurth	32.4
2	Boat of Balliefurth	Craggan-more	27.0
3	Craggan-more	Craigellachie	22.4
4	Craigellachie	Spey Bay	29.2

Suggestions for a 3-day trip

Option 1

Day	From	To	Distance (km)
1	Lochain Uvie	Aviemore	35.3
2	Aviemore	Blacksboat	51.6
3	Blacksboat	Spey Bay	48.1

Option 2

Day	From	To	Distance (km)
1	Aviemore	Grantown	24.6
2	Grantown	Aberlour	41.6
3	Aberlour	Spey Bay	33.5

Option 3

Day	From	To	Distance (km)
1	Kingcraig Church	Grantown	35.9
2	Grantown	Aberlour	41.6
3	Aberlour	Spey Bay	33.5

Distances

Distances between the agreed access points are here if you wish to make up your own itineraries.

Lochain Uvie to Newtonmore	4.8km
Newtonmore to Kingussie	7.2km
Kingussie to Kincraig church	12.0km
Kincraig church to Aviemore	11.3km
Aviemore to Boat of Garten	11.3km
Boat of Garten to Broomhill	6.8km
Broomhill to Boat of Balliefurth	3.0km
Boat of Balliefurth to Grantown	3.5km
Grantown to Cromdale	6.0km
Cromdale to Advie Bridge	11.5km
Advie Bridge to Cragganmore	6.0km
Cragganmore to Blacksboat Bridge	3.5km
Blacksboat Bridge to Knockando	4.0km
Knockando to Carron Bridge	5.3km
Carron Bridge to Aberlour	5.3km
Aberlour to Craigellachie	4.3km
Craigellachie to Boat o' Brig	12.4km
Boat o' Brig to Fochabers	9.4km
Fochabers to Spey Bay	7.4km
Total	**135km**

Looking towards Loch Spey.

📷 Paddling past Ruthven Barracks.

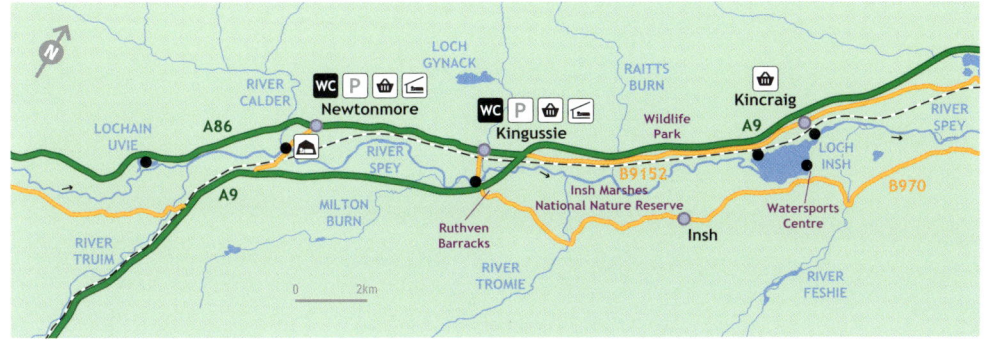

Section 1

Lochain Uvie to Loch Insh

Distance 24km
Start Lochain Uvie, NN 674 957
Finish Kincraig Church car park, NH 838 045
Difficulty Flat water to grade 1 rapids

Agreed access points

Lochain Uvie, NN 674 957 – park in the lay-by at the bottom of the Creag Dhubh crags, access the larger of the two lochs via a small gate (please close this after you). There is a small connecting burn between the lochain and the river where there is a pipe tunnel. If you decide to go through it you must be very aware of the consequences of getting stuck; you can portage round the tunnel on the bank.
Newtonmore, NN 709 980 – access on the river right just below Spey Bridge. If you stay in the Spey Bridge Campsite you may be able to access the river from the campsite.

In Newtonmore please do not leave vehicles and trailers in the lorry park at the Chef's Grill without asking permission.
Kingussie, NN 759 997 – access on the river right below the bridge on the road going to the Ruthven Barracks. Use the gate on the upstream side of the river.
SW Loch Insh, NH 822 043 – use the lay-by opposite the gate lodge and get to the loch by going under the arch by the railway.
Loch Insh Water Sports Centre, NH 837 045 – if you agree launching and landing with them.
Kincraig Church car park, NH 838 045.

Gentle grade 1 after Kingussie.

Nearby attractions

The following attractions are on or just off your route: Ruthven Barracks; Insh Marshes National Nature Reserve; Highland Folk Museum, Newtonmore, Kincraig village shop; Highland Wildlife Park; Loch Insh Water Sports Centre.

Accommodation

The following campsites and hostels are within easy walking distance of the river: Spey Bridge Caravan and Camping Park, Newtonmore; Newtonmore Hostel; Strathspey Mountain Hostel, Newtonmore; Happy Days Hostel, Kingussie; Loch Insh Water Sports Centre, lodges and sometimes camping.

For B&B and hotel accommodation contact the tourist information centre in Aviemore 01479 810930 or Kingussie 01540 661000.

Description

Starting at the lay-by under the Creag Dhubh crags, there is a small gate across the road; use this to access the loch. Make sure that you close any gates that you use. Paddle through the lily pads on the loch and in the far corner there is a small channel with a tunnel that runs into the river. If you decide to portage across to the other loch there is another channel that also runs into the river. From the first loch, if you decide to go through the tunnel to the river rather than portage around it, please be aware of the width and height of you and your boat, and the consequences of getting stuck for whatever reason.

The river here is flat or very slow moving until you see Invertruim House in the distance on the right-hand side of the river. This marks the start of the small grade 1 rapids. The first rapid on a bend turning left is quite congested with trees and islands, and you need to take a bit of care negotiating these in higher water. Thereafter the rapids are all grade 1 riffles, but they keep the interest going for you. The River Truim comes in from the right and this can cause a few waves in bigger water. As you travel further down this section you start to see some really great views down to the Glen Feshie hills and beyond towards Braeriach. The river has some really pleasant easy grade 1 rapids from now onwards and has an open aspect to it. Just before you go under the bridges at Newtonmore you will get a rapid where the River Calder joins the Spey and in bigger water conditions this can have a few good waves; in lower water you need to watch out for the shallow rocks under you. Going under the road bridge at Newtonmore you are at another agreed access point. This one is on the right-hand side of the river just below Spey Bridge. If you are using the campsite you can ask to launch from the campsite on the left-hand side of the river. Many folk choose to start from here if the upper section is too low. Directly following the road bridge there is a railway bridge, and you often see the trains making their way north and south with passengers waving at you as you pass.

From here the river gets a little more congested with fallen trees and tree roots and the rapids, although still grade 1 in technical difficulty, can be a section that you need to take more care on, particularly in higher water levels. There has been some recent clearing of the tree root debris to create a passable channel in the river.

The river flows down past the Newtonmore golf course and if you have an old map you will see a braided section of the river. This has now been cut off and has formed two smaller lochs alongside the river; a good example of an oxbow lake.

Marking the end of Newtonmore is the Allt na Fèithe Buidhe entering from the left, and the railway is again visible. The river then flows onto a more gentle section; this has flood prevention works on the left of the river changing the view of the hills that you get. On the right-hand side as you near Inverton there is a very steep wooded hillside; this is a good marker that you are halfway between Newtonmore and Kingussie. The last few kilometres into Kingussie are fairly gentle with the odd easy

Craig Dubh crags.

Calm water after Kingussie. Photo | Alison Falconbridge.

rapid helping you along. There is another agreed access point just under the bridge on the B970 which runs from Kingussie to Ruthven Barracks and beyond to Insh. This is on the river right; use the gate on the upstream side of the road.

The Ruthven Barracks is a very prominent ruin in a commanding position. It was built between 1719 and 1721, directly after the Jacobite rising in 1715. It is built on the site of an old castle; the first recorded one dating from 1229. The Barracks are well worth an excursion off the river. They are in the condition that they were when they were destroyed in 1746 when another Jacobite uprising set fire to them. Ruthven Barracks are currently maintained by Historic Scotland.

Directly below the bridge in Kingussie there is a gentle rapid that can sweep you into the trees on the left if you don't anticipate it; it is however easy to stay on the right of the river and avoid the trees. From here, continue paddling and you pass under the bridge carrying the busy A9 and onto the slower flowing section with only a few small rapids that goes through the Insh Marshes National Nature Reserve. Insh Marshes is one of the most important wetlands in Europe. It is managed by the RSPB and, depending on the time of year, you may see birdlife such as lapwings, redshanks, snipe, curlews, whooper swans and greylag geese. Between here and Loch Insh you have a wonderful opportunity to observe the birdlife that the reserve is famed for. If you want to explore the marshes rather than just paddling through them, there are marked paths accessible 1km beyond Ruthven Barracks. In higher water conditions it is not unusual to see this whole area under water, and if you choose to paddle you can pass over fields and fences.

When you reach Loch Insh the first of the access points is in the south-west corner of the loch in a lay-by opposite a gate lodge; go under the railway via an arched bridge. The second of the agreed access points is at Loch Insh Water Sports Centre in the north-east corner of the loch (you may be charged to access and egress here, speak to the water sports office when you park). There is a good café at the centre, the cakes come recommended, and they will also sometimes provide camping). The third access point is at Kincraig Church, river right below the church. Please park considerately in the lay-by opposite the church and close the gate when you are through.

As you paddle out of the river mouth coming from Kingussie, paddling the 2km across the loch is usually a joy with the prevailing wind on your back. You may even get the opportunity to get an improvised sail up here to make the most of the winds.

If you paddle to Kincraig Church, the left side of the island (as you look from the Kingussie end of the loch) usually has the deepest water in it and can be paddled at all levels. There is an osprey nest on the north side of the island, and it is recommended that you are quiet when paddling around the island when the birds are likely to be in the area and nesting (usually March to October). Please do not get out on the island around the nesting area.

Kincraig Church is a small community church which, if you are visiting on a Sunday, will usually have a good number of cars in the car park. If you require any provisions it is a short walk over the bridge to the village shop, and there are local pubs in Kincraig for refreshments and evening meals.

Canoeing just below Kincraig Bridge on Loch Insh.

Approaching Aviemore.

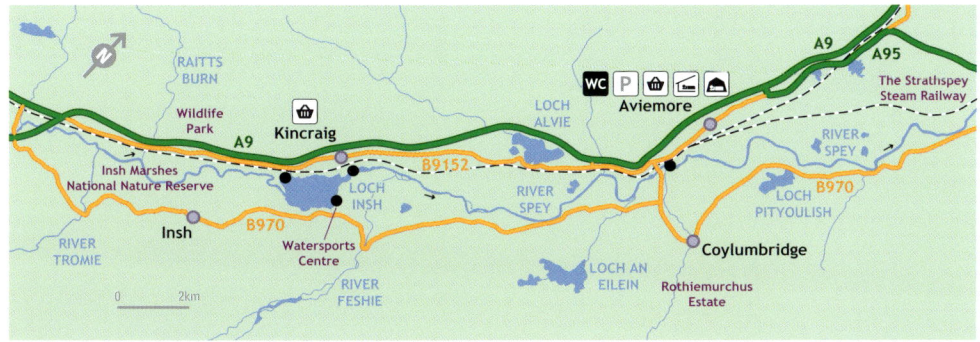

Section 2

Loch Insh to Aviemore

Distance 11.5km
Start Kincraig church car park, NH 838 045
Finish Aviemore Old Bridge Inn riverside car park, NH 894 118
Difficulty Flat water to grade 1 rapids

Agreed access points

Kincraig Church car park, NH 838 045.
Loch Insh Water Sports Centre, NH 837 045 – if you agree launching and landing with them.
South-west Loch Insh, NH 822 043 – use the lay-by opposite the gate lodge. Reach the loch by going under the arch by the railway.
Aviemore Old Bridge Inn riverside car park, NH 894 118.

Nearby attractions

The following attractions are on or just off your route: Kincraig village shop, Highland Wildlife Park, Loch Insh Water Sports Centre, Rothiemurchus Estate, Aviemore village centre.

Accommodation

The following campsites and hostels are within easy walking distance of the river: Loch Insh Water Sports Centre, lodges and sometimes camping; Dalraddy Holiday Park, nr. Aviemore; High Range Touring Caravan and Camping Park, Aviemore; Rothiemurchus Camp and Caravan Park, Coylumbridge; Aviemore Bunkhouse; Aviemore Youth Hostel.

If you fancy staying somewhere quirky try Inshriach House, www.canopyandstars.co.uk. They have a wood-fired sauna and hot tub on the river, and bespoke camping options including a yurt, bothy, beermoth and shepherd's hut, all within easy access to the river.

Sunny and calm Loch Insh.

B&B and hotel information for Kincraig and Aviemore can be found through the tourist information centre in Aviemore 01479 810930 or Kingussie 01540 661000.

Description

Starting from Kincraig Church, you can paddle out into the loch, keeping a careful eye out for the ospreys that often nest on the island. From April until October you are asked to stay off the island to allow them to nest quietly. If you have a pair of binoculars with you it's a great place to watch them soar majestically around the area. If you are lucky, you might even catch a glimpse of them catching a fish or feeding their young in the nest.

The predominant south-westerly winds will often push you across the loch and down into the mouth of the river. As you leave the loch glance at the bridge pillars; they were designed and built at the end of the 19th century and are a lasting legacy to the era, especially considering how high the water flow can go down the River Spey. After the bridge, you can paddle either side of the island. Following the island you come to a bend in the river and this is the start of the flowing section. If you are new to paddling, these first bits of moving water are great places to practise some of the river skills that you will require during your journey; breaking in, breaking out and ferry gliding your boat.

Some gentle flowing water will take you over gravel banks and down towards the confluence of the River Feshie, and the first real grade 1 rapid on this section of river. You can paddle either side of the large gravel island. The main flow usually goes down the left-hand channel. This often has a slightly submerged tree in it and is quite a narrow channel, so if you choose to go this way make sure that you can paddle your boat well enough to avoid the hazards. If you go down the right-hand channel, in low water you may have to walk your boat down the first section where it is shallow. It then deepens and flows past another channel of the Feshie and sometimes some other tree hazards, straight down until the two channels meet again. This junction is a common place to find a number of fishermen. Below this rapid on the left-hand side you can see the riverbank slowly collapsing down the sheer gravel and sandbanks, and the red tin-roofed house situated on top that is getting ever closer to toppling into the river itself. There is another lovely, long, easy rapid with a gravel bank on the right-hand side and a few tree stumps mid-river. This is a really nice place to stop and admire the Glen Feshie hills before you start concentrating on the main bulk of the Cairngorms in front of you.

From here there are a few easy rapids all in gently flowing water until you get to a sharp bend at NH 865 070. There are some pylon lines crossing the river prior to this point, so these are good landmarks to identify the area. This marks another tree hazard, and is sometimes best walked around depending on water levels. You should now start to see Kinrara House and the Duke of Gordon's Monument built in 1836 to commemorate the last Duke of Gordon, which is a prominent landmark on the top of the hill to the left of the river.

When you are under the monument there is another potential tree hazard at NH 884 087. The river continues meandering through the countryside with the Craigellachie hills dominating the landscape in front of you, with the steep grind of the Burma Road etched into its surface; it is a must for fit mountain bikers in the area. To the right you see the solid bulk of the Cairngorm Mountains with the deep cleft of the Lairig Ghru splitting Braeriach from the more commonly visited Cairn Lochain and Cairngorm Mountain area.

You might start to hear the gentle hum of the A9 at this point and see the large pylon lines running alongside the river for a few hundred metres. Don't worry, you quickly turn away from them again, and loop around passing some of the large estate houses of Rothiemurchus, taking you back to that sense of wilderness. As you follow the river you are now getting nearer to Aviemore, and when you travel underneath the large pylon line you know you are almost there. Just a quick rapid with a sharp left-hand bend in it, and you will start to see the new road bridge leading to the ski area, quickly followed by the old bridge, which is now a walking and cycling route.

There is easy access and good parking just after this bridge on the river left in the car park opposite The Old Bridge Inn and the Aviemore Bunkhouse.

Happy paddlers heading towards Boat of Garten.

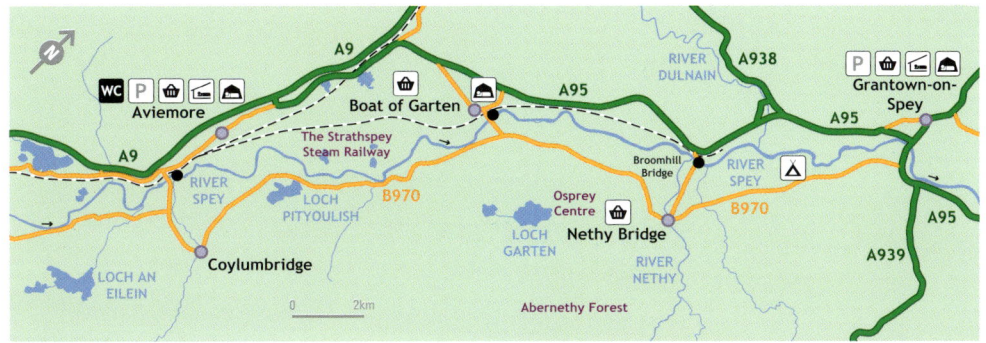

Section 3

Aviemore to Boat of Balliefurth

Distance 21km
Start Old Bridge Inn riverside car park, NH 894 118
Finish Broomhill Bridge, NH 996 224
Difficulty Flat water to grade 1(+) rapids

Agreed access points

Old Bridge Inn riverside car park, NH 894 118. Boat of Garten, parking at the lay-by near to the bridge. Access under the bridge on the left-hand, downstream side, NH 946 191. Broomhill Bridge, parking on the downstream side of the bridge, NH 996 224 – make sure you don't block any access to the river. Access the river on the left under the bridge.

Nearby attractions

The following attractions are on or just off your route: Aviemore village centre, Boat of Garten village, Loch Garten Osprey Centre, The Strathspey Steam Railway, Speyside Wildlife, Nethybridge village.

Accommodation

The following campsites and hostels are within easy walking distance of the river: Aviemore as before, Boat of Garten Caravan and Camping Park, Fraoch Lodge Hostel, Nethy Station Bunkhouse, and Boat of Balliefurth Campsite (marked with a small sign on a pylon saying "Camping this side"). B&B and hotel information for Aviemore and Boat of Garten can be found through the tourist information centre in Aviemore 01479 810930 or Grantown 01479 872242.

Tree debris just after Aviemore.

Sand martin holes.

Description

Leaving the car park at the Old Bridge Inn you are immediately into a section of small rapids that have lots of tree hazards which you need to be very careful of, particularly in bigger water flow conditions.

The River Druie, which you pass on the river right just as you get in, was one of the many smaller tributaries used by loggers in the 17th and 18th centuries.

After you pass the confluence of the River Druie on the right there is a sharp right-hand bend. Although this rapid is an easy one there are usually some tree hazards in the way and the flow can often take you towards the trees, first on the left and then the steep, sandy banking at the bottom of the rapid on the right. Once round the corner there are several more rapids that are similar in nature, many with tree hazards in the river and overhanging trees on the banks where the water flow is taking you. You need to be very aware of them. Staying in the middle of the flow is a good, safe bet here, making decisions to go right or left as you need to. As you pass the steep, sandy banks of the river here, keep a lookout for the small tell-tale holes in the sandbanks which are signs of the sand martin, and which you will see on a regular basis as you are travelling down the river.

Once you have passed the Dalfaber golf course on the left you are onto a much flatter section of river with some lovely scenery surrounding you. Make the most of the Cairngorms and look to the right-hand side of the river every now and then as the hills below you are starting to diminish in size. The Kincardine hills including Meall a' Bhuachaille now form the main skyline on the right-hand side of the river. On the left you have some flatter farmland, and then the smaller hills around Carrbridge come into view.

Just after Kinchurdy Farm, which is on the left-hand side, you will see on the right-hand side of the river, camouflaged into the hillside, a small bungalow with a turf roof, followed by a steep banking with a number of sandy holes in it. If you are travelling here near dusk keep a good lookout for badgers in this area. Highland Badgers will offer you trips out to spot badgers if you are interested.

The start of the rapids is marked by a right-hand bend (NH 937 175) just before you come into Boat of Garten. The run into Boat of Garten has a few rapids that are around grade 1 standard and are generally easy to read from the river. On the right-hand bank you might be able to spot some of the fishing huts for the area. If you are a keen fisherperson you can buy permits for the local area from the Boat of Garten post office.

As you approach Boat of Garten you can see the open fields on the sides of the river and in front of you is a bridge; in 1898 this replaced the ferry that transported people across the river.

Access to the village can be gained just underneath the bridge on the downstream side, and after a short walk uphill into the village you will find: the post office which serves tea, coffee and freshly baked produce; Anderson's restaurant; The Boat Hotel; Dow's Stores; the

Approaching Boat of Garten Bridge.

Boat of Garten Post Office. Photo | Donald Macpherson.

Boat of Garten Caravan and Camping Park; and Fraoch Lodge Hostel.

Putting back onto the water under the bridge the gentle flow takes you off downstream again. In low summer levels watch out for the shallow, gravelly areas on the right-hand side of the main river channel. This next section has a lovely slow flow and generally flat water, where the water meanders along and allows you to paddle through the plains between Boat of Garten and Broomhill, and you usually have to paddle quite a lot compared to the rest of the river. This is the main flat-water section on the river. If the wind is behind you then you may even be able to get a sail up and be blown along the river.

The Strathspey Steam Railway which runs from Aviemore to Broomhill is a good feature to look out for on this section of river, and you get a really good view of any trains running along it with usually a cheery wave from the driver and passengers. As you travel along you will find some old stone bridge pillars in the river. This used to be the crossing for the Strathspey branch of the railway going off to Nethybridge, Grantown, and then onto the North Moray Coast. You can still find the old stations dotted along the Speyside Way if you walk or bike along it.

The first rapid on this section that you will come across is just under the bridge at Broomhill. This rapid can be a little awkward as the flow goes into the bridge pillars at an angle. To get through the pillars safely you need to aim across the flow; generally the middle channel is the easiest. Have a look if you are concerned before you paddle through as it can change with different water levels. You can sometimes in higher water use a small channel on river left missing out the main flow altogether. This is the normal take-out unless you are going on to the campsite just downstream.

After the rapid under the bridge you are back onto easy, just-moving water. As you are paddling along you will see a dense area of forest on the right and following this, a field (again on the right). There are some electricity cables which cross the river at this point and this marks the basic campsite at Boat of Balliefurth (Ronnie and Adelaide Macpherson run this). It is a field with access to a loo. There is an area for a campfire and Ronnie sometimes has some wood that you can use on it, ask first though. To get to their house to pay for the camping, follow the dirt road away from the river and the first house you come across on the left is theirs; it has some beautiful views of the river. They usually have a sign up on the electricity pylon when you land giving their phone number and directions to get to their house. Please don't camp on the opposite bank and use the facilities without paying, they charge very little (currently £3 per person per night).

On the left-hand side of the river in the fields there are three sets of standing stones called Tom Nan Carragh, which is an atmospheric place to explore at sunset. It is thought that it is of Pictish or Druidical origin and appears to be aligned on significant astronomical events.

Heading towards Broomhill Bridge.

📷 Below Grantown.

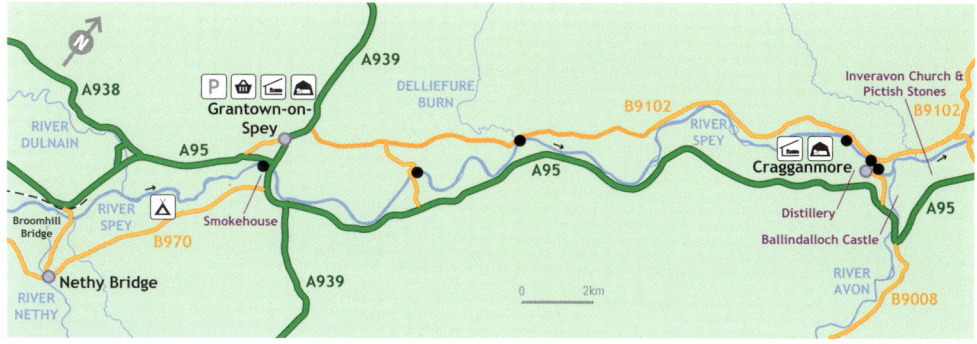

Section 4

Boat of Balliefurth to Cragganmore

Distance 26.5km
Start Grantown-on-Spey, NJ 028 266
Finish Cragganmore Bridge, NJ 169 368
Difficulty Grade 1 and grade 2 rapids

Agreed access points

Grantown-on-Spey, NJ 028 266 – parking spot just off the A95 about 500m above the main road bridge.

Cromdale Church, NJ 066 289 – parking just off the road on the downstream side of the bridge. Access to the river via the track below the bridge.

Delliefure Burn on the left of river, NJ 085 316 – limited parking by the track leading to the fishing hut upstream; be very careful not to block access.

Advie Bridge, NJ 120 354 – left-hand side access via the five-bar gate, parking on verge being careful not to block road.

March Pool, Ballindalloch, NJ 158 369 – left-hand side of river; difficult parking here due to boulders on the side of the road.

Ballindalloch, NJ 167 368 – limited parking on the side of the road. Access is walking via a gate and down a track to the river.

Delnapot/Cragganmore Bridge, NJ 169 368 – just below the bridge on the left-hand side. You can get access to the Speyside Way here which will take you to the camping spot at Cragganmore village.

Enjoying the river.

Nearby attractions

The following attractions are on or just off your route: Grantown-on-Spey village; Anagach Woods; Spey Valley Smoke House, Grantown; Revack Estate; Grantown Museum; Ballindalloch Castle and Gardens; Cragganmore Distillery; Inveravon Pictish Stones.

Accommodation

The following campsites and hostels are within easy walking distance of the river: Ardenbeg Bunkhouse, Grantown; Grantown-on-Spey Caravan and Camping Park; Cromdale Outdoor Centre; Ballindalloch Station Bunkhouse; Ballindalloch Station Campsite at Cragganmore. B&B and hotel information for Grantown to Cragganmore can be found through the tourist information centre in Grantown on 01479 872242 or Dufftown on 01340 820541.

Description

Continuing down the river you start to notice the speed of the river picking up a bit and there are a few easy grade 1 rapids before you get to Grantown. Fishing here is controlled by the Grantown Fishing Association and permits can be bought for different beats in the village of Grantown-on-Spey from Mortimer's shop. This is on the High Street next to the post office.

Marking the edge of Grantown is the old graveyard seen on the left-hand side of the river. There is a small but lovely sandy beach just further down on the left, which gives easy access if you are planning to take out or put in here. From the beach you can see the top of the first of the bigger, longer rapids (around grade 1+ depending on water levels) on the Spey that takes you under the road bridge and down to Grantown Old Bridge. From the top of this rapid just under the road bridge you can see a route down the right-hand side moving left towards a concrete fishing pier. From the fishing pier the river continues straight down and then takes a sharp left-hand bend under the old bridge. In bigger water conditions this rapid may reach grade 2. This is a good fishing spot, and you often get a few fisher folks in this area.

Leaving Grantown Old Bridge you immediately notice that the river has picked up speed and is now going from rapid to rapid. The scenery around you has rounded off and the dominating mass of the Cairngorms on the right-hand side has been replaced by the rolling Cromdale hills. To the left of the river you are passing through Anagach Woods, a beautiful section of Scots pine and carefully managed forest, which is run by the Anagach Woods Trust. If you are lucky you may see crossbills, capercaillie and the elusive pine marten, amongst other rare woodland species.

The rapids from here to Cromdale feel a little more remote than before although the main trunk road, the A95 from Grantown to Elgin, runs close by. The rapids in this section are generally straightforward and are around grade 1(+) depending on water level. Many of the rapids are fairly long as you are travelling down them, and if you are in a group you might need to suggest specific meeting places on the river to regroup. You are also into an area where people pay more for their fishing and you will often see ghillies out with their clients. Some of these may be in the traditional green rowing boats. Make your approach known to people by whistling or a shout of "good day", and ask which way they

Approaching Cromdale Church.

King's Hut.

would like you to pass them. Normally they will ask you to paddle behind them if possible. Most are very pleasant, but if you are the tenth group of paddlers that has passed in the last hour then you can perhaps understand any frustrations shown.

Paddling towards Cromdale Bridge and church you will see a manicured lawn on the right-hand side just in front of the church. This is an agreed access and egress point and a lovely place to stop for a break. The first bridge here at Cromdale was a suspension footbridge built in 1881, and the current road bridge was built in the 1920s. Before this there was a ferry crossing over the river which gave the name Boat of Cromdale, now one of the house names near the river.

Cromdale itself is about 1km up the road on the church side of the river. It is a very small village with big Scottish historic claims to fame. The Battle of Cromdale was fought in this area in 1689, ending one of the Jacobite rebellions, and the Scottish folk song 'The Haughs of Cromdale', supposedly penned after this event, is a very popular tune still.

In low water you might see the remnants of a bird's lunch on the shore in the form of freshwater mussel shells. These are one of the rare sightings found on the River Spey; freshwater pearls were almost fished to extinction and are now a protected species. If you see large quantities of shells in one area, or see people walking in the river with a glass-bottomed bucket, you should report this to the police. See the SCA website for current advice.

Leaving Cromdale Bridge you are again into a section of grade 1(+) water where the flow gently leads you downstream. The river meanders between the busier A95 and the very quiet B9102, neither of which really intrude on your journey. From Dalriach to the farm at Mains of Dalvey there are a few fishing huts. One of the more interesting looking is the King's Hut on the left-hand side of the river. It is a small stone and wood-built hut with antlers adorning it, so called because King Edward VII and various other royalty used to fish here often.

There is a small bridge on the main A95 road over a tributary burn near the farm at Mains of Dalvey which has a set of traffic lights so that only one vehicle can travel at any one time. If you have not been paying attention to the map, this is a good relocation point for you.

After the traffic lights there is a set of islands opposite Culfoichbeg with some fun rapids around them; sometimes these rapids can get a little bigger than grade 1. Following this there is a nice run of gentle rapids down to Advie Bridge.

At Advie Bridge in higher water it is possible to go down the right-hand channel which takes you straight through the bridge, but in lower water levels the main flow tends to go round the left-hand side of the island, which is all fine until you round the last corner just before the bridge. At this point, just before reaching the new bridge on the river left, there are some old submerged bridge pillars that can easily trip a boat up before reaching the eddy line under the bridge. The flow of the current here also takes you towards the new bridge pillars, so this is an area to be aware of. It is worth aiming for the middle gap to avoid the hazards. Once over the excitement of Advie Bridge you can relax and enjoy the river for a while. You are now getting into the area of one of the most paddled sections of the river down to the Knockando rapids. If you lift your eyes from the water you should be now be starting to see the Corbett, Ben Rinnes with granite tors at its summit. The hills to the left of the river are much smaller, and are now home to a wind farm, although the turbines are generally hidden from view here. Between the bridge at Advie and the old railway bridge at Cragganmore there are a number of grade 1+ rapids, which are great to give you a warm-up for the slightly bigger ones still to come. After Advie Bridge you pass a few more grade 1+ rapids before you reach the main access point for this section at the Ballindalloch Pools. There is a second access point in this area. This leads you down a track towards the river and an open field with Cragganmore Bridge below it. At Cragganmore Bridge you can get access to the Speyside Way Campsite, which has basic facilities. Stop just under the bridge on the left-hand side and walk up onto the path on the disused railway. Walk south-west along the railway footpath and you will get to the campsite (approx. 250m). If you have any energy left here you can always go for a walk and discover one of the local distilleries at Cragganmore, go for a quick game of golf up at Ballindalloch Castle Golf Course, walk around the castle grounds, or visit the standing stones at Inveravon.

Approaching Cragganmore Bridge.

Broom in flower.

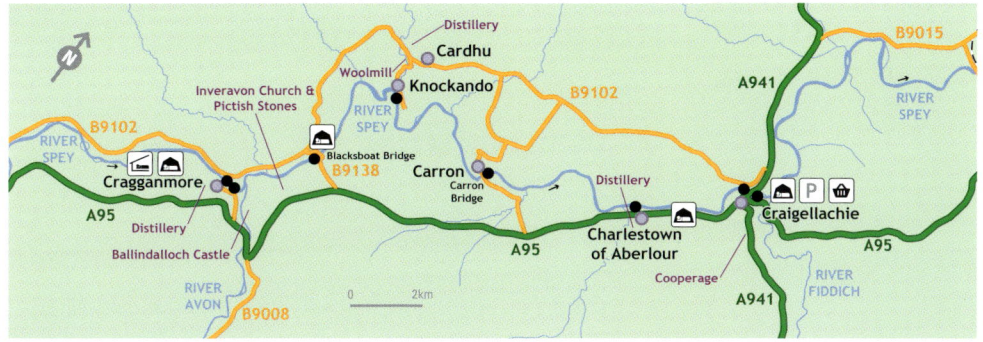

Section 5

Cragganmore to Craigellachie

Distance 21.5km
Start Cragganmore Bridge, NJ 169 368
Finish Craigellachie, NJ 290 452
Difficulty Grade 1 and grade 2 rapids

Agreed access points

Delnapot/Cragganmore Bridge, NJ 169 368 – river left below the railway bridge. If you are starting at the campsite there is possibly parking there.

Cragganmore village, NJ 171 367 – river right, immediately before the houses that are signposted Cragganmore village from the A95. Lay-by on the south side of the B9137. There is a footpath opposite leading to the riverside.

Blacksboat Bridge, NJ 184 389 – river left, just upstream of the bridge.

Knockando, NJ 190 416 – river left below the Tamdhu Distillery. There is parking in the old railway station, and access to the river by the path at the upstream end of the railway platform, passing composting toilets and changing rooms.

Carron Bridge, NJ 225 411 – river left at the bridge. For loading and unloading boats you can use the passing place at the bridge, but please park in the car park in Carron village if leaving the vehicle.

Aberlour, NJ 262 428 – river right on the grassy bank upstream of the Victoria footbridge.

Craigellachie, NJ 285 452 – river right on the sandy beach just below the Thomas Telford bridge. Small car park just next to the beach.

Running the Washing Machine.

Craigellachie, NJ 290 452 – river right near a fishing hut, there is an L-shaped boat park to tie boats to and a quick walk upstream to the Speyside Way. Then turn left on the path and follow it to Fiddich Park where there is good car parking as well as the camp site.

Nearby attractions

The following attractions are on or just off your route: Cardhu Distillery, Knockando Woolmill, Aberlour Distillery, Walkers Shortbread Factory, Speyside Cooperage in Craigellachie.

Accommodation

The following campsites are within easy walking distance of the river: Blacksboat Station camping area, Aberlour Gardens Caravan and Camping Park, Boat o' Fiddich camping area, Craigellachie. For B&B or hotel information contact the tourist information centre in Dufftown on 01340 820541.

Description

This section of the river contains the most regularly paddled water in the guidebook, from Cragganmore to Knockando. The Knockando rapids themselves have an agreed whitewater training section on them. This is agreed with the Knockando Estate in conjunction with the SCA. Due to the high usage, a composting toilet and changing room facility has been built at the Knockando rapids take-out point.

Starting down the river from Cragganmore Bridge, you turn the corner to the left and the river starts to flow more northerly until you reach the confluence of the River Avon (locally pronounced A'an).

In big water conditions the River Avon is one of the main tributaries of the Spey and is one of the reasons why the Spey does not behave like a traditional river, where the closer to the sea you get, the easier the paddle. The Spey picks up pace as it continues downriver, assisted by the water it gains from the Avon and other lower tributaries. The catchment for the Avon is far up in the Cairngorm Mountains. Starting high on the plateau near Ben Macdui, many smaller burns flow into Loch Avon high on the hills. These then drain into the River Avon, which flows remotely through the mountains all the way past Tomintoul and down to the point you are at just now. For more adventurous and skilled paddlers the River Avon from the Tomintoul area down is a great grade 3+ run, and the whole river has in the past been paddled by kayak from Loch Avon down. Getting to Loch Avon and the start of the River Avon involves an epic portage up and over Cairngorm Mountain.

Just after the mouth of the River Avon you get a bigger rapid (grade 2) which turns the corner to the right and leads into another bigger wavetrain. Don't worry if you take on a bit of water here, as there is a calm section and a small beach on the left at which to bail. This is a prime fishing spot, so if there is fishing going on here it is usually best not to linger in the area. If there is no fishing going on it is a lovely rapid at which to practise skills.

After this, another long grade 2 rapid follows the river around a gentle right-hand bend at the top and bounces you down a long straight.

Enjoying the rapids.

There are a number of stone-built fishing piers in this area. At the bottom of the rapid there is an eddy behind a fishing pier on the right-hand side and this is a good stopping point to catch your breath.

The biggest rapid so far is just about to appear. You can usually hear it and it sounds worse than it is. However, it is worth getting out to inspect it if you are concerned. To get out and look it is usually easiest on the river right. The river narrows at the rapid and turns slightly left. In normal water conditions you can't quite see the bottom of the rapid. There is a big, bouncy wavetrain that takes you through the Washing Machine grade 2 (sometimes known as Blacksboat rapid). Following the main part of the rapid, the river stays narrow with a shingle beach for a couple of hundred metres. This channels the water

Top of the Washing Machine.

through quickly, which means that you need to plan your break-out and be very active in your paddling to make it. In low water the rapid is actually steeper than in high water, when it fills in and widens out below, over the shingle bank. You will often need to bail your boat after the Washing Machine. This is easily done on the shingle bank river right at the bottom of the rapid.

Following this, the river takes you into a gentle rapid with a lovely playspot on the right, and continues down towards Blacksboat Bridge where there is access just above the bridge on the left. You can walk from here to the campsite at Blacksboat camping area. There are no facilities here other than running, cold water. Walkers and bikers on the Speyside Way use this camping spot as well.

There is a lovely fishing hut just underneath the bridge and the anglers are keen that you pull in at the access point on the upstream side of the bridge if you need to do so, rather than in front of their hut. Please phone the estate on **01807 500205** to let them know that you will be leaving boats on the river bank.

Blacksboat Bridge (originally the site of another ferry) is followed by Craigroy Island which is normally taken by following the line on the left-hand side with a lovely grade 1+ rapid. At NJ 181 410 you will see an estate sign on the right-hand bank requesting that paddlers stay to the right-hand side; this is a very popular fishing pool.

Round the corner from here you get to another island. In higher water levels you can paddle either side of this, but in lower water, it gets very shallow on the right, although it is usually possible to paddle. The left-hand channel has some tight moves around a tree and boulder at the top of the rapid, and then flows into a pleasant, bouncy wavetrain. There is a sign on the left-hand side of the river asking you to stay on the right-hand side of the river. This is part of a local river users' agreement with the landowners.

You are now at the top of the Knockando rapids, grade 2, which are probably the most well-known rapids on the river. Here, river levels depending, you have a choice of routes. In higher water you can shoot either side of the next island, but in lower water, or if you are wanting the more technical route down in high water, you should go down the left-hand side of the main islands round the outside of the bend.

At the top of the rapid at Knockando on the right-hand side you will see there is a white post on the bank. This marks the top of the whitewater training area, and there is a similar post opposite the put-in point at the bottom of the rapid. Knockando Estate agreed to this designation, and you can train and paddle between these posts between 10am and 10pm. There is a portage trail on the right-hand bank of the river (opposite side to the car parking and toilet). On the left-hand side on the riverbank there is good parking, a composting toilet, and basic male and female changing rooms. Coming down to the river from the car parking area there are some steep steps that go down passing the toilet; paddlers are requested to use these rather than the older steps slightly further down the rapid. When using the composting toilet you are requested to put a handful of sawdust down the hole after, but nothing else as other items do not compost down. Note that nobody is employed to clean the changing rooms and toilets, however, the local RAF centre and Glenmore Lodge do a good job of raking the compost below and replenishing the sawdust in the bin above. Please leave the toilets and changing area as clean as possible.

Leaving Knockando rapids you are again into a series of longer grade 1+ to 2 rapids, you will normally go down the right-hand side of Roary Island, and this leads you round to the next major rapid on a right-hand bend at NJ 210 420. It is another rapid where you have to get quite close to the top to actually see down. It is big and bouncy grade 2 with a large wavetrain at most water levels. At low water you

Composting toilets at Knockando.

Top of the Knockando rapid in low water.

normally have to start the rapid on the left and move right through the flow. From here you have some lovely scenery and pass through a few more easy-to-read rapids. Soon you will start seeing the chimneys of the derelict Imperial Distillery on the left-hand side. There is a sharp left-hand bend in the river and this leads you round and under the majestic arches of the bridge at Carron.

From Carron Bridge to Victoria Bridge in Charlestown of Aberlour there are some great grade 1 and 2 rapids. Keep your eyes open for one that has a bit more oomph to it at NJ 243 426. It is a long grade 2 rapid with a large wave near the top. Depending on water levels you can usually skirt around it to the right or left, but if you go through it can easily swamp a boat. At the bottom of the first section of rapids there is a second rapid that flows around a left-hand corner. From this point the rapids become a bit easier again taking you down towards Aberlour.

The Victoria Bridge at Aberlour is a footbridge that crosses the River Spey and is locally known as the Penny Bridge after the toll that was once charged to cross it.

Aberlour was originally famous for its orphanage which closed in 1967, but is now mostly famous for its two main industries which are whisky and shortbread. Walkers have had a shortbread factory there for over 100 years and you often get a lovely smell wafting over the river as you paddle past. There are about 50 whisky distilleries within a 15 mile radius of Aberlour, some of which you have already paddled past.

From Aberlour to Craigellachie there is a section of grade 1+ rapids keeping things moving along. By now you will be so used to them that you probably are not noticing them quite so much. As you approach Craigellachie, you get a superb view of the Thomas Telford designed bridge, completed in 1815. Its iron arch spans the river and is still open to pedestrians and cyclists although not to vehicles; a new road bridge was built slightly downstream. You can get access to the river just below the bridge on the right where there is a lovely sandy beach with a small car park. If you are planning to camp here then you should continue down the river under the new road bridge, and about 500m further on the right-hand side there is a small, black fishing hut just above the confluence of the Fiddich Water (NJ 289 452). Pull in below here and you will see an L-shaped boat rack where you can lock up your boats overnight. To get to the campsite, walk towards the fishing hut and you will see some steps which lead you up to the main Speyside Way. Turn left (downstream) on this path, go through a gate and walk under a stone-arched road bridge until you reach Fiddich Park car park, where you will find a basic toilet block and water pipe. The camping area here (free) is just beyond the car park and is signposted on the left-hand side. It is a lovely flat area behind a raised, grassy earth bank. Although Craigellachie is a small village, there are a few hotels with a superb selection of Speyside whiskies in them; it is worth sampling a few of them during an evening here.

Paddling past Penny Bridge at Aberlour.

Otters Hole.

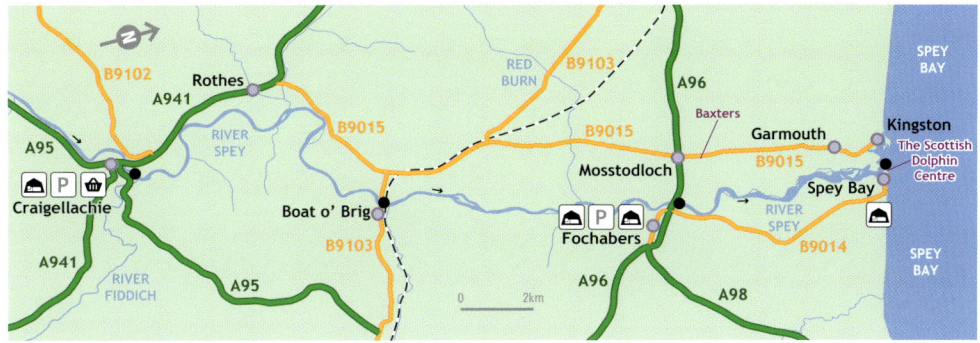

Section 6

Craigellachie to Spey Bay

Distance   28km
Start   Craigellachie, NJ 290 452
Finish   Spey Bay, NJ 348 654
Difficulty   Grade 1 and grade 2 rapids

Agreed access points

Craigellachie, NJ 290 452 – river right near a fishing hut, there is an L-shaped boat park to tie boats to and a quick walk upstream to the Speyside Way. Then turn left on the path and follow it to Fiddich Park where there is good car parking as well as the camp site.

Boat o' Brig, NJ 318 517 – river left at the bridge, access via the track leading past the water board building. There is a small car park between the bridges.

Fochabers, NJ 341 595 – river right, below the road bridge. The parking lay by is situated on the Spey Bay road (B9104) giving access to a track to the river.

Spey Bay, NJ 348 654 – river right next to the buildings and car park, marked as Tugnet on the map.

Nearby attractions

Baxters, Fochabers, The Scottish Dolphin Centre, Spey Bay.

Accommodation

The following campsites are within easy walking distance of the river: Burnside Caravan Park, Fochabers. Spey Bay Golf Club and Caravan Site. For B&B and hotel accommodation contact Elgin Tourist Information Centre on 01343 562608.

Near Craigellachie Bridge.

Description

As you leaving the riverbank at Craigellachie, stay on the right-hand side, if possible, until you are at the next rapid. Enjoy the last day of paddling. You are gong to pass through some superb scenery and beautifully manicured lawns of fishing estates and huts. The river continues dropping downhill at a great rate and continues offering you rapids of grade 1 to 2 throughout the day.

At the island opposite Rothes (NJ 286 498) there is often a tree (or tree debris) which overhangs the main low water channel on the left-hand side. This means that this is an area to be very aware of, particularly in low water where you are channelled very close to the edge of the island. From here down you continue meandering along the river from rapid to rapid (all grade 1 to 2, but very easy to read) .

Just before you arrive at Boat o' Brig, there is a rapid at NJ 312 506. This has a nasty boulder in the middle of the river which should be avoided; it has been the scene of many upsets in a canoe. The river then continues from one easy rapid to the next until you get to the road and rail bridges at Boat o' Brig.

Haugh Island is your next decision, you can go down either side, but again be aware of tree debris that can collect in this area. Just below here you have some stunning crags along the right riverbank, and another good rapid where the river funnels through a smaller gap. Then the land opens out again until you reach the Orton earth pillars (sometimes known as the Seven Pillars of Hercules) which are red, clay pillars sticking out into the river. There is a small recirculating eddy near one of them that can have you going around for a wee while in high water. You can also sometimes get some strong gusts of wind around the cliffs in this area. When you see the huge power lines crossing above the river you have 3km to go until you reach Fochabers.

The run into Fochabers has a few interesting rapids on it with two to note. Just after the huge sandstone cliffs at NJ 339 575 (again look out for the sand martin colonies that inhabit here), there are two large rock dykes in the water on the right-hand side, these are a major hazard to a paddler. Make sure you give them a wide berth on their left-hand side. There is then another right-hand bend rapid, and then after a few more rapids you turn another sharp corner to the left coming towards Fochabers. Here, particularly in low water, you have to be active in your paddling to avoid the wall and the trees. You then follow the river into the final section to the bridges at Fochabers. You can get access onto the river just below the bridge here. At this point you can often smell what is cooking in the Baxters' factory. The factory shop has a good cake stop and is just a short walk from here.

Between Fochabers and Spey Bay the river changes on a regular basis, with tree debris getting washed down and the gravel banks changing the river flow each flood. The rapids are still mostly around grade 1 to 2 depending on the water level, and in high water this section can be quite exciting and dangerous due to the debris.

Lunch stop below the Orton earth pillars.

The old railway bridge near Garmouth is a really convenient marker that gives you a 1km warning until you reach Spey Bay. There is often tree debris caught on the bridge pillars, so care is required here. This is now used as part of the Moray Coastal Path and you can sometimes see walkers and cyclists travelling across it. If you have chosen to do your shuttle by public transport you will walk across the bridge to get to the village of Garmouth.

This last section of the Spey generally has a lot of fishing going on and it sometimes feels like a slalom course, working out which is the best line down through all of the islands and avoiding the folks fishing. Occasionally if you get the wrong line in low water you may end up having to jump out and portage across to a different channel; don't worry, all of the flowing channels will lead you towards the sea, some go a bit more directly or more easily than others. Often you can see ospreys flying and fishing in the area, which is a real treat at the end of the trip.

When you get to the point that you can see the buildings at Tugnet and further onto the open sea, you know you have completed a really special journey. Far away on the left-hand side of the river you can see Kingston and Garmouth. These were once the major shipping ports that took all of the logs that came from further up the river, off down south. Originally Garmouth was the port, then over the years the river moved away and the port changed to Kingston. Kingston was also a popular ship building port in the late 1700s to late 1800s.

As you reach the lagoons near the sea you start to feel the effect of the tide on your journey, and if you dip your hand into the water at certain points of the tide it is starting to taste salty.

Check the tides for your planned day of arrival at Spey Bay; if the tide is going out when you arrive then be aware of this as you paddle down the last section. Tidal flow and river water make a strong current flowing out of the lagoons and it can be difficult to get back into the shore, especially if there is an offshore wind blowing. If you have tide and river flowing out with an onshore wind (northerly), you can get a line of breaking waves to go through which can be quite daunting as well. When the tide is coming in, and is pushing against the flow of the river, you can again get a line of breaking waves near the mouth of the river. At slack tide and low winds it can be absolutely lovely to get out into the sea and have a short paddle out there to complete your journey. As you return to shore, the river flow often creates an eddy for you to cross when you come back into the lagoon area.

Even if you decide not to go out onto the sea there is a lovely feel to the area at Tugnet and Spey Bay. The shingle banks are beautiful to look at and wander across. On the shingle banks of the shore here there are many remnants of the tree debris that has floated down the river. Most of the logs are bleached by the sunshine and weather. You get frequent sightings of seals, dolphins and occasionally whales in the area.

The buildings at Tugnet started off life as part of the fishing station, including a domed ice-house to preserve the salmon caught when they used to net the river and catch everything that was going up. Some of these buildings have now been converted into the Moray Firth Wildlife Centre, which is part of the Whale and Dolphin Conservation Society. They also house a great café for well-earned tea and cakes at the end of your journey. If you want to stay at the seaside for your final night, a campsite has recently opened at the Spey Bay Golf Course near the old Spey Bay Hotel. The journey down the River Spey is a magical paddle, coming from the high mountains through the long Strathspey with majestic scenery surrounding you, travelling through villages and towns, taking in the history as you go, the mountains gradually shrinking and disappearing as you reach the sea. It is a journey to savour and enjoy throughout. I hope you have as much fun on the river as I do.

Paddling across the lagoons.

Standing up to see the next rapid.

Safety and Rescue

Being able to look after yourself, and the other boats and people that you are travelling down the river with, is a really important skill. There are many good books and DVDs on the subject, so I will just highlight a few things.

- Wear appropriate safety kit including a buoyancy aid and helmet, and carry a river knife and safety gear.

- Make sure you have you boat kitted out with buoyancy bags, swim lines (open canoe), and have a spare throw bag.

- Inspect rapids if you are unfamiliar with them before going down them, either by standing up in the boat and having a look, or by walking down the bank to check them out.

- Learn to read a rapid before you go down it so that you can choose to take the dry line or safe route, therefore reducing the chance of capsizing or swamping your boat.

- Learn how to use a throw bag and to rescue a canoe (or your chosen craft) before you go, so if it does all go wrong you have practised it beforehand.

Try reading
White Water Safety and Rescue by Franco Ferrero
BCU Canoe and Kayak Handbook which has a chapter on safety and rescue

Try watching
White Water Safety DVD by Bruce Jolliffe and Dougie Shannon

Paddling towards fishermen.

Access, Wild Camping and Fishing

In Scotland we have The Scottish Outdoor Access Code. This code gives us a good explanation of our rights to accessing the countryside, but also states that with those rights comes responsibility and we need to recognise this when we are paddling or getting to the river. You can find more information at www.outdooraccess-scotland.com.

The three key principles of the code are: take responsibility for your own actions, respect the interests of others, and care for the environment. One of the main other river user groups on the River Spey is anglers, and a good rapport has been built up between the angling community and regular river users over the years. Dave Craig, the current SCA River Adviser for the Spey, has been a key player in forming and maintaining the Spey Users Group, which meets on a regular basis to address any issues that have arisen on the water or on the riverbanks. He is a good contact to chat to about any updates on and off the river. Dave can be contacted on 01540 673826 and davecraig1@btinternet.com.

Wild camping

Although in this guide I have suggested routes that start from recognised campsites, there are many beautiful wild camp spots on the Spey, particularly on some of the islands and riverbanks close beside the river. To stay within the framework of the Scottish Access Code you should keep your group small, camp away from houses or roads, ensure adequate toilet facilities are used (this may be a trowel), and you should aim to leave your campsite with no trace of you being there. There is a paddlers' wild camping guide on the Scottish Canoe Association (SCA) website which contains very useful information.

📷 *Leaving no trace.*

Toileting

If you are going to the toilet out of doors there are some basic guidelines that should be followed. Go to the toilet a minimum of 30m away from the river, with care and consideration for others and the environment. This means burying or taking out any waste. If burying faeces please do so a minimum of 15cm below the soil level to allow proper decomposition. Please do not leave any visible evidence of your visit; toilet paper especially dries in warm weather and can then blow about and get into the river. Any sanitary products should be taken out, as they do not biodegrade. I have a toilet kit that I take with me on camping journeys which is in an identified dry bag and contains a trowel, toilet paper, zip lock bags for toilet paper and sanitary items, and gel hand wash.

Campfires

Campfires can be lit in suitable sites (away from any vegetation or trees) making sure that you leave no evidence of your fire. A firebox is ideal to use, or have your fire on a shingle beach or sandbank where you will be able grind up any left over ash so it will disperse more easily. If this is not possible, then lifting a turf and then replacing it afterwards is an alternative.

For more ideas on minimising our impact as we travel down the river try contacting the 'Leave No Trace' organisation on www.lnt.org. The above sections on toileting and campfires are two of the seven principles of their leave no trace policy.

📷 *Responsible camping kelly kettle.*
Photo | Donald Macpherson.

Fishing

The River Spey is one of Scotland's top salmon fishing rivers as well as being a must for paddlers. The fishing season is between 11th February and 30th September which covers the prime paddling time. With this in mind the SCA and the Spey Fishery Board issued a Spey Anglers Guidance for when kayaks and canoes approach.

The SCA also has a leaflet detailing a Paddlers' Access Code, which asks us to keep an eye out for anglers. The key principles are as follows. If you see someone fishing think about how it is best to pass them with the least disturbance. Where possible it is best to stop upstream and attract the angler's attention before passing, this is best done with a whistle. If they have a line in the water, wait for a signal to proceed and then follow the route that they indicate, if safe and practical to do so. An angler should point to the side they want you to pass by on. Many anglers wading in the water will want you to paddle behind them. It is also asked that

Passing behind a fisherman.

you identify yourself to anglers or landowners if requested; anglers should reciprocate if asked by you.

There are an increasing number of boats paddling on the river, and ideally the fishing and paddling community can continue the positive dialogue that has been happening over the past number of years. For this to continue it needs both anglers and paddlers to be aware of the others' needs, and to try to accommodate them as best as possible. So as a paddler, be aware that although you may have been having an amazing wilderness experience, the angler that you pass may have already seen several groups of boats passing them throughout the day, which may detract from their overall experience on the river. A cheery smile, a wave and a "hello" often go a long way to help the situation.

If you do have a problem there are a number of ways of reporting it. For a serious problem contact the police. The SCA have an online form that is used for reporting incidents, and you can also contact the local access officer for the area. From Laggan to Dellifure Burn contact the Cairngorm National Park Outdoor Access Team on 01479 873535. For the Tulchan Estate contact the Highland Council Access Officer, Stuart Easthaugh on 01463 255287, and from Ballindalloch to Spey Bay contact the Moray Council Local Access Officer, Ian Douglas 01343 557049.

Fishing on the lower stretches of the Spey.

Spey Anglers Guidance

Anglers can reasonably expect:

- The leader of the paddling group will endeavour to ensure the angler is aware of their presence by either shouting or ideally blowing a whistle (most likely to be heard over water noise).

- Once contact is established the leader will seek information on the angler's preferred line of passage for the group.

- Paddlers will wish to cause minimum disturbance to the angler's direction of casting and, water depth/obstructions allowing, paddlers will move in the direction indicated. Where the angler is standing on the bank, direction indicated may include towards the angler, even under the rod, or towards the opposite bank. If the angler is wading, canoeists will be very happy, where possible, to pass behind, i.e. between the angler and the bank.

- Leaders will endeavour to have their group pass in fairly close formation, with a reasonable, safe distance between each boat, thus minimising the time taken to pass.

- If an angler is playing a fish, paddlers normally wait upstream until the fish is landed or until there is indication from the angler or ghillie that it is safe to pass towards the direction indicated.

- In the event of inadvertent capsize, paddlers will do utmost to affect efficient rescue and refloat upturned canoe as soon as possible. Currents can catch out even the most experienced paddlers!

- Once past, the party will continue on their way downstream. Paddlers will not loiter unnecessarily or play in a pool where someone is actually fishing.

Anglers are requested to:

- Acknowledge they are aware of the presence of paddlers.
- Carefully consider which line is most practical for both angler and paddler.
- Give clear direction as to the preferred side for the craft to pass.
- Not always necessary to take in line. However, refrain from casting while boats pass by.
- As soon as the boats have safely passed, the angler may very soon resume fishing.

Sailing past an osprey nest on Loch Insh.

Wildlife

For me, a huge part of the joy of travelling down the River Spey is what I see when I am passing by. There are numerous creatures that live in the river and on the riverbanks and they, alongside the wildflowers and trees, help to characterise the river as being a great wilderness journey. Some of the most regularly spotted creatures you might see are:

In the water

Salmon

Salmon are regularly seen leaping when you are paddling the River Spey, and they are the reason that most of the anglers are standing on the side of the river. Salmon spawn and hatch in gravel banks in fresh water. Once large enough (they will stay up to 3 years where they were hatched) they migrate down to the sea, and then return to the River Spey between one to four years later to complete the cycle and spawn themselves. Salmon are a member of the trout family. Other species that you might also find in the River Spey are brown trout and sea trout. Salmon regularly leap out of the water and you may be lucky enough to see this at close quarters. A once-in-a-lifetime experience is to have a salmon jump over your boat, or as happened to one client on the river, have one jump out of the water and hit your buoyancy aid. We all turned round wondering what the huge shout and clatter was – it had knocked him off his seat before bouncing back into the water!

Bottlenose dolphins

The Moray Firth is the home of a group of bottlenose dolphins that travel around the East Coast. They are grey in colour with a darker back and dorsal fin and are up to 4m long. Dolphins usually travel round in schools or pods, so you are likely to see a few at a time. They are often sighted at Spey Bay, but for a more guaranteed sighting pop along to

Dolphin at Chanonry Point. Photo | istockphoto.com.

Chanonry Point as they go there to feed. The Scottish Dolphin Centre is at Spey Bay and they will help you spot dolphins and other coastal wildlife.

Seals

Both common and grey seals are spotted in the Moray Firth and they fish around the mouth of the River Spey. Common seals are slightly smaller than the grey seals, they tend to have a darker coat with a longer nose, and it is often said they look a bit like a dog. The grey seals are the largest UK seal, and can be told apart by their distinctive roman-style nose, and their coat which is often blotchy grey, brown and black.

Minke whales

Minke whales are a small whale which are occasionally seen on the coast around the mouth of the River Spey. Their body is usually dark on the top with a lighter belly, they are around 7m to 11m in length, and their dorsal fin is quite tall, being positioned about two-thirds of the way along their back. They have a very graceful slow, deep dive.

On the land

Red squirrels

The red squirrel is native to Britain and is a fairly common sighting in and around the woodlands surrounding the River Spey. They are often seen in the trees on the riverbank and have a red-brown coat with a white tummy and little tufts of fur coming out of their ears. You can sometimes hear them shouting at you with a distinctive 'chuk chuk' noise and perhaps a bit of foot stomping. I think perhaps one of the most wonderful sightings that I have had of squirrels on the River Spey was when I watched them swimming across the river using their tail as a rudder. It took a while to recognise what the animal was, as I had not expected to see them doing that.

Otters

Otters are elusive creatures but are seen regularly in the early morning or late evening on the River Spey. They are territorial and like to live in areas of undisturbed undergrowth on the riverbank. They mark their territory with their droppings, which you may come across if you are exploring the riverbank thoroughly. You might also find a worn patch on the riverbank where an otter has been regularly getting in and out. The Spey has a healthy population of otters. This is thought to be a reflection of the good habitat for them, such as reed beds, islands, and a plentiful food supply.

Wild cat

Known as the 'Tiger of the Highlands' you will be very lucky to catch a glimpse of a true wild cat. There are many sightings that prove to be the offspring of feral cats who have at some point mated with a wild cat. It is estimated that there are around 100 genuine wild cats left in the area. Their coat is black with brown stripes, with a very muscular body, and a thick tail with

Red squirrel. Photo | istockphoto.com.

Otter. Photo | istockphoto.com.

Pine marten. Photo | istockphoto.com.

Roe deer. Photo | istockphoto.com.

a blunt black tip. If you want to guarantee a sighting, go the Highland Wildlife Park where they are helping with a breeding programme.

Pine marten

Pine martens are becoming a more common sighting around the Badenoch and Strathspey area. They are of similar size to a cat, with dark brown fur and a white throat. They are members of the weasel family and are a protected species. You will often see them in wooded areas where they eat other small mammals, fruits and berries. In areas where they are frequent sightings many people attract them into their gardens by feeding them; they seem to have a fondness for jam and peanut butter.

Red and roe deer

Higher up the river there are some herds of red deer that roam around. They are common sightings around Loch Spey and down to Laggan. Red deer have the typical stag heads that you see adorning an estate house wall. They have a reddish-brown to brown coloured coat which will turn more greyish in the winter. They are around 110cm to 120cm at the shoulder on average. The stags have large antlers with many branches, the older they get the bigger the antlers. They have been recorded living up to 18 years old.

There are also many roe deer in the area and you will often find them in forested areas. They have a lighter, reddish-brown coat, which turns pale brown in the winter. They are very much smaller than red deer, being about 60cm to 75cm at the shoulder.

Badgers

Seldom seen in daylight, the badger is an easily recognisable animal with its dark grey body and black and white striped head. They are social animals and live in networks of tunnels called setts. They have a fierce reputation, however their favourite food is earthworms. They have short, powerful legs for digging out their setts and foraging for food. They are around 90cm in length and are commonly known in Scotland by the name 'Brock'.

Osprey. Photo | istockphoto.com.

Buzzard. Photo | istockphoto.com.

In the air

Osprey
Seen from below the osprey has a white breast. It has long graceful wings with a black elbow joint and wing tips. The osprey has a wing shape similar to a gull and is often mistaken for one, however it is a much larger bird and once closer is easy to distinguish. It is an amazing sight to see one swooping down to grab a fish and then fly off with it grasped firmly in its talons. You can see ospreys at any point along the River Spey, but good places to regularly see them are; Rothiemurchus Fishery, Loch Insh where there is a nest on the island (do not land there between April and October), Loch Garten where there is a camera trained in on an osprey nest, and the last section of the river at Spey Bay.

Buzzard
Buzzards are commonly found all along the banks of the River Spey. It is a large bird having broad, rounded wings with 'fingers' on the ends of their wing tips. They have a large fan-like tail. Their back is brown, and seen from below they have a lighter coloured breast with a dark leading edge of the wings. You will often spot them when you are doing the shuttle as well as when you are on the river, as they like to sit on fence posts and survey the land around them.

Sand martin
Sand martins are very small birds, wintering in Africa and making the flight back over to Scotland and the River Spey in spring each year. They have dark brown upper bodies, and dark under their wings with very white tummies. They are very agile fliers catching insects over the water. They create their homes in the sandy riverbanks, and you will often see a collection of holes high in the sand cliffs which you will see on your journey down the river. They flit in and out of these with insects for their young.

Heron. Photo | istockphoto.com.

Dipper. Photo | istockphoto.com.

Goldeneye duck

These are a medium-sized diving duck with a distinctive yellow eye. The males are black and white with a green head, and the females are smaller with a grey-brown head. They nest in trees, or in specially constructed boxes, and the young, once ready, jump down and into the water. When you see the height that the nest boxes are placed it seems a daunting prospect to jump and land safely. They however do it, and seem to be making a success of it, as there appears to be an increasing number of them on the River Spey.

Mallard

The mallard is one of the most common ducks found on the River Spey. They are a relatively large duck. The male is stunning with his green head, yellow bill and dark body with a little curl to his tail. The female is less bright with her feathers being flecked brown and having a more brown-coloured beak. You will often see lines of chicks following their mothers around in the spring and summer months.

There are not so many brightly coloured males in the summer, they moult and start looking a similar colour to the female for part of the summer until they get back into their breeding plumage.

Grey herons

Grey herons are one of the most commonly seen birds on the river. They are very tall with long legs, a long beak and are predominantly grey in colour with some black and white feathers as well. They often look prehistoric when they take off and can remind people of a pterodactyl with long, slow flaps of their huge wings. Herons nest in trees and hunt in the River Spey, with fish and frogs being some of their favourites. They tend to harpoon their prey with their long beak and may walk very slowly, or be absolutely still, when hunting.

Dippers

Dippers are beautiful, small, plump birds with a black or dark body and a white chest. They

Capercaillie. Photo | istockphoto.com.

Crossbill. Photo | istockphoto.com.

have a very distinctive bobbing motion. You will often see them sitting on rocks in the middle of the River Spey. Occasionally, if you are really lucky, you might see them walking into the water or swimming underwater to feed. They feed on insects found in the water, and may also eat fish eggs or small fish.

Capercaillie

A huge grouse-like bird with a spectacular tail in the breeding season. Commonly spotted in the forests surrounding the River Spey above and below Aviemore. If you want to watch the lek (mating display) in its full glory, the Loch Garten Nature Reserve run a Capercaillie watch in April and May. They are quite rare in the UK, so a treat to watch.

Goosander

These birds have a serrated bill (sawbill family) making them look like they have teeth which they use to catch and eat fish. They are a handsome bird with black and white plumage, a green head and a red-coloured beak. You will often see them racing along the riverside running on the water. In the late spring and early summer you will see whole families hiding underneath the foliage on the riverbanks.

Red-breasted merganser

These are another of the sawbill family with the goosander. Another fish-eating duck. The males are black and white with a green tufted head and a browny-red chest, the female is grey with a browny-red tufted head, and both have a red beak.

Crossbill

These are sometimes seen in the scots pine woodlands in the Badenoch and Strathspey area. They are a large finch that often flock together eating seeds from pine cones as they go. Males are a distinctive red-orange colour and females are more yellow-green with grey-brown. Their bill has a distinctive curve to allow them to get the pine seeds out.

Group about to get off the river

Environmental Issues

There are a number of environmental issues that are starting to become more prevalent. At each of the agreed access points you will find a sign that has been put up highlighting *Gyrodactylus salaris* and signal crayfish. These ask you to ensure that if you have been paddling, fishing, or in the water in another river or country, then to make sure that your boat, equipment and personal kit has been thoroughly washed.

Gyrodactylus salaris is a salmon parasite, which is found at present in large quantities in Scandinavia, it is also found in other European salmon rivers. It is vitally important to river ecology and economy that this parasite is not brought into the UK as it could have a devastating effect on rivers.

Signal crayfish are from North America and have established themselves in the UK. At present they are just found in England and the south of Scotland. They eat a wide range of species and have a particular fondness for fish eggs, which again could have a huge impact on the fish stocks and other areas of the ecology of the River Spey.

Freshwater mussels are a protected species, which have a recovering population in the River Spey. At one point they were almost fished to extinction for the freshwater pearls that they contain. If you see anybody acting suspiciously, for example walking in the water with a glass-bottomed bucket, or come across large quantities of the shells, you should report it to the police and the National Wildlife Crime Unit; use the number 101 to report it, or 999 in an emergency case.

Sign on the river.

Train pulling into Boat of Garten station.

History of the River Spey

The River Spey has a long history of people working, travelling down it, and living along its shores, from the Pictish settlements evidenced by their standing stones, all the way through to our more recent recreational uses of the River Spey for canoeing and kayaking. In the 1970s Clive Freshwater from Loch Insh Watersports Centre won navigation rights for paddlers down the river, which has benefited us all greatly. More recently the River Spey has been designated a Core Path in the Cairngorms National Park Authority. I have added in a few bits of information here, but there are many more interesting stories to be found in other publications. I have certainly enjoyed researching them.

Logging

In the 1700s there were a number of logging businesses on and around the River Spey. Timber was cut in the forests of Nethy Bridge, Glenmore and Rothiemurcus and transported to the nearest running water source where they built small dams. You can still find remains of some of these dams in the Glenmore Forest area. When there was a suitable amount of logs in the burn, the men would open the dams and send them down to the Spey where they were caught and stored until made into a raft and floated to the sea. They were originally stopped at the port of Garmouth, but later on the port changed to Kingston as the river changed direction. There was much ship building on the coast, and the logs were loaded onto the ships and transported to many towns in the south of Scotland and England, particularly London.

At the mouth of the River Druie, one of the Spey tributaries that floated the logs down from Rothiemurcus and Glenmore, there was a basic bothy which was specifically for the logging men. Most of the men were from the coastal areas and had no other accommodation in the area. The men all knew the river well, and would wait in the bothy until they had enough logs to create their rafts and send them downstream. They would then return to it after they had walked or ridden back to Aviemore to start making the next one. There are no remains of the bothy now.

Originally men in currachs (large coracles) would guide the logs and rafts down river; there are records of this from the Rothiemurcus Estate dating back to the 1500s. In the 1700s the style of rafting the logs changed to building a larger raft that had planks on top, allowing two men to steer it. The river was 'improved' to allow rafts to flow down it more easily. This involved removing obstacles such as boulders. In the late 1700s there was a court case in Edinburgh where it was claimed that the log rafts were damaging fishing on the river. The court upheld the use of the rafts and they were allowed to continue.

There were also a number of sawmills and boring mills in the area. There is still a house called the Boring Mill in the Rothiemurcus area. This was used to drill holes in very straight logs for water pipes. Many of these went down to London to help with sanitation issues there. Logging and rafting like this had largely stopped by the early 1800s. There is a lovely description of the logging trade in 'Memoirs of a Highland Lady' by Elizabeth Grant.

Whisky and distilleries

A huge number of whiskies are distilled in the area surrounding the River Spey, and it is one of the industries that has stood the test of time. Up until 1820 there were no legal distilleries in the area, although there was apparently no shortage of whisky either. It is suggested that there were up to 200 illegal distilleries in the area. After the Excise Act in 1823, distilleries in the area became recognised, although there are records that the excise men still managed to uncover illicit stills every now and then. Whisky has gone from strength to strength in the area, each one praising the water that it uses to make its Uisgebaugh (water of life). There are a number of very good distillery tours in the area for those wanting to know more and to sample some of the unique flavours produced in the area.

Railways

It is not unusual to see a steam train puffing along the tracks when you are travelling from Aviemore to Broomhill Bridge; the best views from the river are usually between Boat of Garten and Broomhill Bridge, where you often get a friendly wave from the train driver and passengers.

There were two train lines in the area. The train from Perth and further south originally came up over Drumochter, onto Dalwhinnie, and through the villages to Aviemore, Boat of Garten, Broomhill, Grantown-on-Spey, Dava and up to Forres where it joined up with the line going to Inverness. It was originally known as the Highland Line. It is now known as the Strathspey Steam Railway.

At Boat of Garten there was a second line built and this was the Strathspey Line. It ran parallel to the Highland Railway and then went over the river to Nethy Bridge (you can still see the bridge pillars on the river), and from there follows what is now the Speyside Way up towards Craigellachie where it met the Keith to Dufftown lines and Elgin to Lossiemouth lines. It was opened in 1863 and became a tourist trip for many folks taking a day out, as well as transporting whisky, sheep, cattle, and other freight. It passed through many of the stations that are now camp spots or recognised access and egress points for us as paddlers. You will see many bikers and walkers following the long distance route that is the Speyside Way mostly following the railway line from Buckie, through Spey Bay and up to Aviemore. You may even meet a few of them in the Speyside Way campsites if you use them.

Farming and droving

Crofting in the Badenoch and Strathspey area has had a long history. The Highland Folk Museum in Newtonmore gives a very good picture of life in Badenoch and Strathspey, with croft houses and other industries in the area set up to show life through the past. It was a hard and basic lifestyle with most folks being tenant farmers. In the times of the clearances many people were driven off the land in favour of sheep, although not all moved away from the area. The villages grew bigger as people relocated down to them and worked locally.

Many of the traditional drove roads from further up in the Highlands came through the Badenoch and Strathspey area, and were used by people taking cattle to the markets or trysts in Crieff and Falkirk, and possibly even further south. There were good pastures in the area which encouraged the drovers to stop for a break here allowing the animals to rest before taking the journey over Drumochter further south. The book 'The Drove Roads of Scotland' gives a very good account of some of these meetings in the area.

Salmon fishing at Spey Bay

Until the 1940s salmon fishing at Spey Bay was a commercial activity employing over 100 people at its height. The salmon were caught in large nets which were rowed upstream and across the estuary, left for a while, and then brought in by hand. The fish were then dispatched by the fishermen onshore and taken off to the ice-houses for storage, before being transported to market, often in London.

At Tugnet you can see the three domes of the ice-houses, where the salmon, once caught, were stored. In the winter, the ice from the river was stored in the insulated ice-houses and used to preserve the fish for transportation. In winter and spring it was possible to send fish all the way to London before they became spoiled. Later on in the summer, when the ice had melted, they used a different method of preserving the salmon. The salmon were boiled in vinegar and then salted, and this kept them good in the heat of the summer. You can see the boilers and read more about the history of the ice-houses at the Dolphin Centre.

Near Fochabers.

Navigation Skills for the River

Navigation and map reading skills are really useful to have when you are paddling down a river. They will help you find the put-in and take-out points and, if you need to identify where you are for any reason, relocation skills will help you with that. A GPS is a fantastic addition to your kit to do this, however it is also very useful to be able to read a map just in case the batteries run out. As an alternative to a GPS unit, many smartphones have useful GPS or mapping apps on them.

Grid references

When you know where you are on a map you can give an accurate position. This is called a grid reference. In the UK we have a great mapping system which splits the country down into 100km blocks. Each block is given a unique double letter, which are found on the map. If you are printing off a map from any computer based mapping programme, make sure that you print off the double letters. If you ever have to contact the emergency services, you will be asked for them.

These 100km blocks are then split down into 1km grid squares that we see on a map. The grid lines mark out each of these 1km blocks and each grid line has a number.

From this you can easily identify where you are by giving the double letter (which is the 100km identification) and the relevant numbers.

For example, on the map below, if you want to identify the square that shows Carron Bridge, you start with the letters NJ (on OS sheet 28 Elgin & Dufftown).

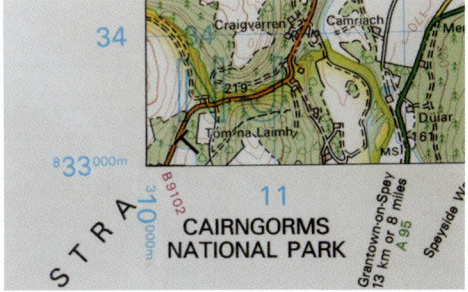

The double letter identification on a map - NJ.

Now you take the number of the grid line along the western edge of the square, found along the bottom of the map sheet (22), and then the number of the grid line along the southern edge of the square, seen at the side of the map (41), and that will give you a 4-figure grid reference, NJ 2241.

To make the grid reference even more accurate you can split the 1km square down into 10 equal squares across the bottom of the square and 10 up the side of the square. This now gives you a 100m square. So the 6-figure grid reference at Carron Bridge would be NJ 225 412.

If you use a GPS it will normally come up with an 8-figure grid reference, which being within a 10m square is even more accurate again. It may also have a location position on a map if you are using a GPS with maps loaded into it.

The 4-figure grid reference for Carron Bridge - NJ 2241.

Using the scale on a compass to get a 6-figure grid reference for Carron Bridge - NJ225 412.

Rafting on Loch Insh, with a map close to hand.

Using features to identify where you are

To help make sure you know where you are when on the river, here are some top tips.

- Have your map folded to the correct area, waterproof it and attach it to the boat or to you so you can see it during the day.
- At the start of the day, pick out any features that you will definitely see when you are travelling down the river, and tick them off in your head as you are journeying past. For example the section from Cragganmore to Craigellachie, "I am going to pass the confluence of the River Avon, Blacksboat Bridge, the islands at Knockando with some tight bends on the river, Carron Bridge, the bridge at Charleston of Aberlour and the two bridges at Craigellachie. Ben Rinnes should go from being in front of me, to be at the side of me, and then behind me, and then possibly out of sight."
- Time how fast you are paddling on different flows of water and this can help you estimate how long a section will take. Between 4km to 6 km per hour is a good estimate if travelling continuously. This obviously depends on the flow of the river.

Relocation skills

If you do not know where you are, some basic relocation skills for use on the river are helpful.

- Take your last known point and estimate how long you have paddled from there.
- Are there any easily identifiable features beside the river, for example: bends in the river, bridges, buildings, tops of hills, etc. You may have to go ashore to find this.
- You can take a bearing down the river and see which direction it is going in. To do this you need to point your compass downstream and line up your compass with the edge of the river. Keep the compass flat and away from any metal in your boat or in your buoyancy aid. Turn the dial round until the floating red needle is hovering above the hatched red arrow on your compass and then add on any variation (currently around 3.5 degrees on sheet 28). Then you can put the compass onto the map and without moving the dial, line up the grid lines with the north/south lines on the compass.
- You should find that in some places on the map the edge of the river should match the direction that the compass is pointing. This limits the number of places where you can be, and using the other skills you can narrow it down further.
- Ideally if you keep an eye on the map throughout the day you should be able to continually see where you are and it should be easy to identify your location.

Index

A

Aberlour 53, 58, 59
Aberlour Distillery 54
Access 69
Accommodation 32, 37, 41, 48, 54, 61
Advie Bridge 47, 50
Anagach Woods 48, 49
Anagach Woods Trust 49
Aviemore 37, 39, 41
Avon, River 54, 55

B

Badgers 42, 78
Ballindalloch 47
Ballindalloch Castle 48
Ballindalloch Castle Golf Course 51
Ballindalloch Pools 51
Battle of Cromdale 50
Baxters 61, 63
Blacksboat Bridge 53, 56
Blacksboat Rapid 55
Boat o' Brig 61, 62
Boat of Balliefurth 41, 47
Boat of Balliefurth Campsite 45
Boat of Cromdale 50
Boat of Garten 41, 43
Broomhill 44
Broomhill Bridge 41, 44
Buzzard 79

C

Campfires 70
Capercaillie 49, 81
Cardhu Distillery 54
Carron Bridge 53, 58
Cragganmore 47, 53
Cragganmore Bridge 47, 51, 53, 54
Cragganmore Distillery 48
Craigellachie 53, 59, 61, 62
Craigroy Island 56
Crayfish 83
Creag Dhubh 25, 31, 32
Cromdale 50
Cromdale Bridge 50
Cromdale Church 47, 50
Crossbill 49, 81
Culfoichbeg 50

D

Dalfaber golf course 42
Dalriach 50
Deer 78
Dippers 80
Distances 29
Distilleries 86
Dolphins 64, 75
Droving 87
Duke of Gordon's Monument 39

E

Environmental issues 83
Equipment 15
Equipment list 18

F

Farming 87
Fiddich Park 54, 59
Fiddich Water 59
Fishing 49, 64, 69, 71, 72, 87
Fochabers 61, 63
Freshwater mussel 50, 83

G

Garmouth 64
Garva Bridge 23
Goldeneye duck 80
Goosander 81
Grantown Fishing Association 48
Grantown Museum 48
Grantown Old Bridge 49
Grantown-on-Spey 47, 48
Grid references 89
Group paddling 13
Gyrodactylus salaris 83

H

Haugh Island 62
Heron 80
Highland Badgers 43
Highland Folk Museum 32, 87
Highland Line 86
Highland Wildlife Park 32, 37, 78
History of the River Spey 85

I

Imperial Distillery 58
Insh Marshes National Nature Reserve 32, 34
Inveravon Pictish Stones 48
Invertruim House 32
Itineraries 27

K

Kinchurdy Farm 43
Kincraig Church 31, 35, 37, 38
King's Hut 50
Kingston 64
Kingussie 31, 34
Kinrara House 39
Knockando 53
Knockando rapids 51, 54, 57, 58
Knockando Woolmill 54

L

Laggan 24
Laggan Bridge 24
Lagoons 64
Lochain Uvie 23, 25, 31
Loch Avon 55
Loch Garten Osprey Centre 41
Loch Insh 31, 35, 37
Loch Insh Water Sports Centre 31, 32, 35, 37
Loch Spey 23
Logging 85

M

Mains of Dalvey 50
Mallard 80
Monadhliath Mountains 23
Moray Firth Wildlife Centre 65

N

Navigation skills 89
Nethybridge 41
Newtonmore 31, 32, 33

O

Old Bridge Inn, Aviemore 37, 39, 41, 42
Orton earth pillars 62
Osprey 38, 79
Osprey Centre, Loch Garten 41
Otter 77

P

Packing a canoe/kayak 15
Paddlers Access Code 71
Parasite (salmon) 83
Penny Bridge 58, 59
Pine marten 49, 78
Planning 13, 27

R

Railways 86
Red-breasted merganser 81
Rescue 67
Revack Estate 48
River Avon 54, 55
River levels 19, 20
River Spey, Upper 23
Roary Island 57
Rothes 62
Rothiemurchus 39
Rothiemurchus Estate 37
Ruthven Barracks 31, 32, 34

S

Safety and rescue 67
Salmon 75
Salmon parasite 83
Sand martin 42, 63, 79
Scottish Dolphin Centre 61, 76
Scottish Outdoor Access Code 69
Seals 64, 76
Seven Pillars of Hercules 62
Shuttles 14
Signal crayfish 83
Spey Anglers Guidance 71, 73
Spey Bay Golf Course 65
Spey Bay (Tugnet) 61, 64
Spey Bridge 31, 33
Spey Bridge Campsite 31
Spey Dam 24
Speyside Cooperage 54
Speyside Way campsite 51
Speyside Wildlife 41
Spey Valley Smoke House 48
Squirrels 77
Strathspey Steam Railway 41, 44, 86

T

Tamdhu Distillery 53
The Haughs of Cromdale 50
Toileting 70
Tomintoul 55
Tom Nan Carragh 45
Tugnet 61, 64, 65

U

Upper River Spey 23

V

Victoria Bridge 58

W

Walkers Shortbread Factory 54
Washing Machine Rapid 56
Weather 19
Whale and Dolphin Conservation Society 65
Whales 64, 76
Whisky 86
Wild camping 69
Wild cats 77
Wildlife 75

Spirit of the Spey

OPEN CANOE JOURNEYS
With Spey Specialist Dave Craig

Canoe Journeys ~ Whisky Tours ~ Coaching Sessions
01540 673 826 • 0787 033 8110
www.spiritofthespey.co.uk

beyond ADVENTURE

Guided River Spey canoe trips
Shuttles & canoe/kayak transport
Canoe hire & outfitting service

t: 01887 829202
e: email@beyondadventure.co.uk
w: beyondadventure.co.uk